trotman

D0528356

GETTING INTO

Medical School

2008 entry

12th edition

James Burnett

Getting into Medical School

This 12th edition published in 2007 by Trotman, an imprint of Crimson Publishing, Richmond, Surrey TW9 2ND

© Joe Ruston, 1996; Joe Ruston and James Burnett 1998, 2000, 2001, 2002, 2003, 2004, 2005, 2006; James Burnett 2007

Editorial and Publishing Team
Authors James Burnett
Editorial Mina Patria, Publishing Director; Jo Jacomb, Editorial Manager; Jessica Spencer, Development Editor; Ian Turner, Production Editor
Production John O'Toole, Operations Manager
Advertising Sarah Talbot, Advertising Manager (020 8334 1617)

British Library Cataloguing in Publication Data
A catalogue record for this book is available from the British Library

ISBN 978 1 84455 141 5

All rights reserved. No part of this publication may be reproduced, stored in a retrieval system or transmitted in any form or by any means, electronic and mechanical, photocopying, recording or otherwise without prior permission of Trotman.

Typeset by Ian Turner

Printed and bound in Great Britain by Creative Print & Design (Wales) Ltd

Contents

For up-to-date information on
medicine and medical schools, go to
www.mpw.co.uk/getintomed

Acknowledgements

Thank you to Joe Ruston who wrote the early editions of this book. It was Joe's idea to write a book aimed at helping prospective medics and so without him neither this title nor the others in the *Getting into* series would exist.

In order to write this book, I have needed to get help from many sources. Without the help of the medical schools' admissions departments, this book would not exist, and I would like to record my gratitude to all of the people who gave up their time to answer my questions. I am very grateful to Sally Billingham at King Edward VI School in Edgbaston, Fiona Pyrgos at Bryanston, Joyce Smart, Sheri Newman and Joanna White from the HIV charity Positive East, and Maya Waterstone and Sam Kirkwood for their help and support.

Finally, I would like to thank the many students and doctors who have provided me with interview questions, factual material and encouragement.

James Burnett
February 2007

INTRODUCTION

A REALISTIC CHANCE

Approximately two out of every five students applying for 2006 entry to medical school gained a place. Many of those who were rejected were excellent candidates with good GCSE results, high predicted A level grades and a genuine belief that medicine was the right career for them. So why were they unsuccessful? Clearly, not everyone who wants to become a doctor can get into medical school because there are a fixed number of places available. However, many good candidates do not give themselves a realistic chance of getting an interview because their preparation is not as thorough as it ought to be. If you are to prepare effectively for your application, you need to start early – ideally two years before you are due to submit it to UCAS. However, even in a short period of time – a few months – you can put together a convincing application if you follow the advice in this book.

UCAS statistics for the 2007 application cycle show that applications have decreased by about 3% compared to last year. By the October 15 deadline, UCAS had received about 15,500 applications from UK students and another 3,500 from EU and other overseas students. There are fewer than 8,000 places available at medical schools so more than half of the applicants are going to be disappointed.

THE GRADES YOU NEED

Table 2 (page 116) shows that, with a few exceptions, the A level grades you need for medicine are AAB. You might be lucky and get an offer of ABB but you will not know that until six months before the exams and you can't rely on it. As a general guide, candidates offering qualifications other than A level are likely to need the following:

- **Scottish:** ABB in Advanced Highers
- **International Baccalaureate:** around 35 points including 6,6,5 at Higher Level (including Chemistry)
- **European Baccalaureate:** minimum of about 70% overall, with at least 80% in Chemistry and another Full Option science/mathematical subject.

BUT THERE'S MORE TO IT THAN GRADES...

If getting a place to study medicine was purely a matter of achieving the right grades, the medical schools would demand AAA at A level (or equivalent) and ten A* grades at GCSE, and they would not bother to interview. However, to become a successful doctor requires many skills, academic and otherwise, and it is the job of the admissions staff to try to identify which of the thousands of applicants are the most suitable. It would be misleading to say that anyone, with enough effort, could become a doctor, but it is important for candidates who have the potential to succeed to make the best use of their applications.

NON-STANDARD APPLICATIONS

Not all of the successful applicants were applying during their final year of A levels. Some had retaken their exams, while others had used a gap year to add substance to their UCAS application. Again, it would be wrong to say that anyone who reapplies will automatically get a place, but good candidates should not assume that rejection first time round means the end of their career aspirations.

Gaining a place as a retake student or as a second-time applicant is not as easy as it used to be, but candidates who can demonstrate genuine commitment alongside the right personal and academic qualities still have a good chance of success if they go about their applications in the right way. The admissions staff at the medical schools tend to be extremely helpful and, except at the busiest times of the year when they simply do not have the time, they will give advice and encouragement to suitable applicants.

ADMISSIONS

The medical schools make strenuous efforts to maintain fair selection procedures: UCAS applications are generally seen by more than one selector, interview panels are given strict guidelines about what they can (and cannot) ask; and most make available detailed statistics about the backgrounds of the students they interview. Above all, admissions staff will tell you that they are looking for good all-rounders who can communicate effectively with others, are academically able and are genuinely enthusiastic about medicine: if you think that this sounds like you, then read on!

ABOUT THIS BOOK

First of all, a note on terminology. Throughout this guide, the term 'medical school' includes the university departments of medicine. Secondly, entry requirements have been quoted in AS and A level terms; a general guide to the grades or scores that you need if you are taking Scottish Highers, the International Baccalaureate or other qualifications can be found on page 2.

Would-be doctors face three major obstacles:

- Getting an interview at medical school
- Getting a conditional offer
- Getting the right A level grades.

The main body of this book is divided into sections covering each of these three major activities.

Most medical schools consider and accept mature candidates, graduates, applicants from abroad, those who studied arts subjects at A level and those who have had to retake their A levels. If you are in one of these categories you will need to read pages 69–78.

A number of other excellent books are available on the subject of getting into medical school. Suggestions for further research are included in Chapter 6. The difference between these other books and this one is that this guide is a route map; it tells you the path to follow if you want to be a doctor. To that extent it is rather bossy and dictatorial. We make no apologies for this because we have seen far too many aspiring medical students who took the wrong subjects, who didn't bother to find work experience and who never asked themselves why they wanted to be a doctor before their interview. Their path into medicine was made unnecessarily difficult because they didn't prepare properly.

Finally, the views expressed in this book, though informed by conversation with staff at medical schools and elsewhere, are our own.

James Burnett
February 2007

1

GETTING AN INTERVIEW

You need an interview because most medical schools issue conditional offers only after their admissions panel has met you. The evidence that the selector uses when he or she makes the choice to call you for interview or reject you is your UCAS application. Some sections of the application are purely factual (your name, address, exam results, etc). There is also a section where you enter your choice of medical schools. The personal statement section gives you an opportunity to write about yourself and there is a space for your teacher to write a reference describing your strengths and weaknesses. Later in this book, you will find advice on how to fill in these sections and how to influence your referee, but first let's consider what happens, or might happen, to your application.

Typically, a medical school might receive 2,500 UCAS applications, almost all of which will arrive in September and October. The applications are distributed to the selectors, who have to decide which applicants to recommend for interview. The selectors will usually be busy doctors, and the task of selecting promising candidates means a good deal of extra work for them, on top of the usual demands of their full-time jobs. Most of the candidates will have been predicted grades that will allow them to be considered, but the medical school can only interview, perhaps, 25% of them.

A high proportion of applicants will have good GCSE and AS results and predicted grades at A level of ABB or higher, and will have undertaken some voluntary work or work-shadowing. In order to decide who should be called for interview, the selectors will have to make a decision based solely on the information provided by you and your school. If you are not called for interview, you will not be offered a place at this medical school. If your UCAS application does not convince the selector that you are the right sort of person to be a doctor, he or she will reject you. However outstanding your personal qualities are, unless your UCAS application is convincing, you will not be called for interview. This part of the guide is designed to maximise your chances of getting the interview even under the worst circumstances.

DECIDING WHERE TO APPLY

There are 32 medical schools or university departments of medicine in the UK. They offer a range of options for students wishing to study medicine:

- Five- or six-year MB BS or MB ChB courses (UCAS codes A100 or A106)
- Four-year accelerated graduate-entry courses (A101 or A102)
- Six-year courses that include a 'pre-med' year (A103 or A104)

Entry requirements of all medical schools are summarised in Table 2 (page 116).

Oxbridge is in a separate category because, if getting into most medical schools is difficult, entry into Oxford and Cambridge is even more so (the extra hurdles facing students wishing to apply to Oxford or Cambridge are discussed in *Getting into Oxford & Cambridge*, another guide in this series). The general advice given here applies also to Oxbridge but the competition is intense and before you include either university on your UCAS application you need to be confident that you can achieve three A grades at A level and that you will interview well. You should discuss an application to Oxford or Cambridge with your teachers at an early stage.

Although you can apply to five institutions, you may only apply to four medical schools: if you enter more than four, your UCAS application will be rejected.

The question is: what should you do with the other slot? The medical schools will assure you that you can apply for other, non-medical, courses without jeopardising your application to medicine, but we would advise you to think carefully before doing so, for the following reasons:

■ There's no point in thinking about alternatives if you really want to become a doctor.
■ If you are unlucky and receive no conditional offers for medicine, you could feel yourself obliged to accept an offer from your 'insurance' course. This will make it impossible for you to accept a place for medicine through Clearing. (Clearing, in case you haven't heard about it, is the process whereby the places of those who were given conditional offers but didn't get the required A level grades are shared out among those who didn't get the conditional offers but did get the grades. The system is described on page 60.)
■ You might find it harder to convince your interviewers that you are completely committed to a career in medicine if you appear to be happy to accept a place to study, say, Chemical Engineering or Archaeology.

The one reason to put a non-medical choice on your form is if you are not prepared to wait a year if your application is unsuccessful, and you intend to enter medicine as a graduate (see page 70).

So, you need to select four medical schools. In deciding which ones to eliminate, you may find the following points helpful.

- **Grades and retakes:** If you are worried that you will not achieve ABB/AAB grades the first time round, include at least three schools that accept retake candidates (see Table 2, page 116). The reason for this is that if you make a good impression at interview this year you may not need to face a second interview at your next attempt. You will also be able to show loyalty by applying twice to the same school. Many medical schools will consider second-time applicants only if they applied to them originally.

- **Interviews:** A few medical schools do not interview A level candidates. If you think that you will be a much stronger candidate on your application form than in person, it may be advantageous to include these schools. Each school's interview rates are shown in Table 1.

- **Location and socialising:** You may be attracted to the idea of being at a university rather than at one of the London medical schools which are not located on the campuses of their affiliated universities. One reason for this may be that you would like to mix with students from a wide variety of disciplines and that you will enjoy the intellectual and social cross-fertilisation. The trouble with this theory is that medical students work longer hours than most other students and tend to form a clique – so be warned: in reality you could find that you have little time to mix with non-medics.

- **Course structure:** While all the medical schools are well-equipped and provide a high standard of teaching, there are real differences in the way the courses are taught and examined. Specifically, the majority offer an 'integrated course' in which students see patients at an early stage and certainly before the formal clinical part of the course. The other main distinction is between systems-based courses, which teach medicine in terms of the body's systems (eg the cardiovascular system), and subject-based courses, which teach in terms of the fundamental subjects (anatomy, biochemistry, etc).

- **Teaching style:** The style of teaching can also vary from place to place. In particular, some medical schools use problem-based learning (PBL) extensively. For example, the course at East Anglia features PBL and the programme offers a variety of formats to encourage learning, including whole-class discussions, lectures, seminars and, especially, small-group sessions. Clinical, communication and IT skills are taught throughout. Within each year, clinical experience is provided in general practice and in hospitals. Assessment is on a unit-by-unit basis and includes: multiple-choice questionnaires; portfolios, presentations and projects; 'advance notice' questions in which researched answers are presented under examination conditions and Objective Structured Clinical Examinations (OSCEs). These are matters of personal preference.

- **Intercalated degrees and electives:** Another difference in the courses offered concerns the opportunities for an intercalated Honours BSc and electives. The intercalated BSc scheme allows students to tack one further year of study either to the end of the two-year pre-clinical course, or as an integrated part of a six-year course. Successful completion of this year, which may be used to study a wide variety of subjects, confers a BSc degree qualification. Electives are periods of work experience away from the medical school and, in some cases, abroad.

- **Oxbridge:** Oxford and Cambridge are special cases. You can apply only to one and your teachers will advise you whether to apply to either. You would need a good reason to apply to Oxbridge against the advice of your teachers and it certainly is not worth applying on the 'off chance' of getting in. By doing so you will simply waste one of your valuable four choices.

You should consult the prospectus of each medical school in your own school's careers library. Once you have narrowed the choice down to about 10–12, it is worth writing to all those on your list for a copy of each prospectus (these will be sent to you free of charge) and taking a good look at their websites.

WHAT THE SELECTOR LOOKS FOR

Most medical schools use a form which the selector fills in as he or she reads through your application. Have a look at the example on the next page; the next part of the chapter will examine each heading on this form in more detail.

MEDICAL INTERVIEW SELECTION FORM

Name	UCAS number
Age at entry	Gap year?
Selector	Date

SELECTION CRITERIA COMMENTS

1| Academic (score out of 10)

GCSE results

AS grades/A level predictions

UKCAT/BMAT result

2| Commitment (score out of 10)

Genuine interest in medicine?

Relevant work experience?

Community involvement?

3| Personal (score out of 10)

Range of interests?

Involvement in school activities?

Achievements and/or leadership?

Referee supports application?

Total score (maximum of 30):

Recommendation of selector	Interview	Score 25–30
	Reserve list	Score 16–24
	Rejection	Score 0–15

Further comments (if any)

**ACADEMIC
ABILITY**

GCSE RESULTS: POINTS TOTAL AND BREADTH OF SUBJECTS

By the time you read this you will probably have chosen your GCSE subjects or even taken them. If you have not, here are some points to bear in mind:

- Medical school selectors like to see breadth. Try to take as many GCSE subjects as possible. Try to take at least eight but if your school places restrictions on the choice or number of GCSEs you take, make sure this fact is referred to in your confidential reference.

- You will almost certainly need to study two science/maths subjects at A level and you will need to study Chemistry. There is a big gap between GCSE and A level. If you have the choice, don't make that jump even harder by studying combined or integrated science rather than the single science subjects. If your school will not allow you to study the single subjects, you should consider taking extra lessons during the summer holiday after your GCSE exams.

- Medical school selectors look at applicants' GCSE grades in considerable detail. Many medical schools ask for a 'good' set of GCSE results. What does this mean? Well, it varies from university to university, but a minimum of five A/B grades plus a good grade in English Language GCSE is likely to be required. Most medical schools will require higher than this. Some medical schools specify the grades that they require, whilst others use the points system (see www.dfes.gov.uk/performancetables/nscoringsys.shtml for more information).

- If you have already taken your GCSEs and achieved disappointing grades, you must resign yourself to working exceptionally hard from the first day of your A level course. You will also need to convince your UCAS referee that the GCSE grades are not an indicator of low grades at A level, so that this can be mentioned in your reference.

AS LEVEL GRADES / A LEVEL PREDICTIONS

AS LEVELS: DO THEY MATTER?
Under the old A level system, the first year of the sixth form (year 12) could be a time for adjustment, contemplation and relaxation. Even if you studied modular A levels, the marks did not feature on your UCAS application, and modules could be retaken again and again. The new system puts pressure on you from the start since not only do the grades appear on your application, but also many of the medical schools will specify minimum grade requirements. Even those that don't will consciously or subconsciously use them as an indicator of your likely A level grades. Imagine the situation: the selector has one more interview slot to fill, and has the choice between two students with identical work experience, GCSE results and A level predictions; but one has scored DDDD at AS level, the other achieved AAAA. Who do you think will get the place? The other thing to bear in mind is that a score of DDDD is unlikely to lead to AAB at A level since an AS contributes 50% of the total A level marks, and so the selectors may doubt that the predicted grades (see below) are achievable. You must be aware of the importance of retaking AS units if possible. Every extra mark gained on the (easier) AS units is a mark that you don't have to get in the (harder) A2 exams. If you have a second attempt at an AS unit, the board will take the higher of the two marks.

A LEVEL PREDICTIONS: DOES YOUR SCHOOL EXPECT AT LEAST ABB?

Your choice of A levels
You will see from Table 2 that most medical schools now ask for just two science/maths subjects at A level, with another science at AS level. They all require Chemistry and/or Biology so you need to choose either Physics or Mathematics if you wish to apply to a medical school that requires three science/maths subjects. There are three important considerations.

- Choose subjects that you are good at. You must be capable of an A grade. If you aren't sure, ask your teachers.
- Choose subjects that will help you in your medical course: life at medical school is tough enough as it is without having to learn new subjects from scratch.
- While it is acceptable to choose a non-scientific third AS or A level which you enjoy and which will provide you with an interesting topic of conversation at your interview, you should be careful not to choose subjects such as art which are practical rather than academic. General studies is not acceptable either. However, students who can cope with the differing demands of arts and sciences at A level have an advantage in that they can demonstrate breadth.

So what combination of subjects should you choose? In addition to Chemistry/Biology and another science at A level, you might also consider subjects such as Psychology, Sociology or a language at AS level. The point to bear in mind when you are making your choices is that you need high grades, so do not pick a subject that sounds interesting, such as Italian, if you are not good at languages. Similarly, although an AS level in Statistics might look good on your UCAS application, you will not do well at it if you struggled at GCSE Mathematics. You will need to check the individual requirements, but in general it is likely that most medical schools will prefer at least one AS level to be in an arts or humanities subject.

Taking four A levels

There's no harm in doing more than three A levels or four AS levels, but you should drop the fourth/fifth subject if there is any danger of it pulling down your grades in the others. The medical schools will not include the fourth A level in any conditional offers they make.

The prediction

The selector will look for a grade prediction in the reference that your teacher writes about you. Your teacher will probably make a prediction based on the reports of your subject teachers, your GCSE grades and, most importantly, on the results of the school exams and AS levels that you take at the end of Year 12.

Consequently, it is vital that you work hard during the first year of A levels. Only by doing so will you get the reference you need. If there is any reason or excuse to explain why you did badly at GCSE or did not work hard in Year 12, you must make sure that the teacher writing your reference knows about it and includes it in the reference. The most common reasons for poor performance are illness and problems at home (eg illness of a close relation or family breakdown).

The bottom line is that you need to persuade your school that you are on track for grades of at least ABB. Convincing everyone else usually involves convincing yourself!

APTITUDE TESTS

BMAT

Students applying to study medicine at Cambridge, Imperial, Oxford and UCL are required to sit the BioMedical Admissions Test (BMAT). The test, which takes place in November, consists of three sections:

1 | Aptitude and skills (60 minutes – 35 multiple choice or short-answer questions)
2 | Scientific knowledge and applications (30 minutes – 27 multiple-choice or short-answer questions)
3 | Writing task (30 minutes – one from a choice of three short essay questions).

Further details can be found on www.bmat.org.uk.

UKCAT

Twenty-four medical schools in the UK require applicants to sit the UK Clinical Aptitude Test (UKCAT). The institutions that require UKCAT are Aberdeen, Brighton and Sussex, Cardiff, Dundee, Durham, East Anglia, Edinburgh, Glasgow, Hull York Medical School, Keele,

King's College London, Leeds, Leicester, Manchester, Newcastle, Nottingham, Oxford (graduate-entry medical degree), Peninsula Medical School, Queen Mary, Queen's Belfast, Sheffield, Southampton, St Andrews and St George's.

For 2007 entry, the test lasted 90 minutes and assessed aptitude rather than academic achievement. The test comprised four multiple choice sections:

1 | Verbal reasoning
2 | Quantitative reasoning
3 | Abstract reasoning
4 | Decision analysis.

For 2008 entry, the test may be expanded to include some extended writing. Additional information, and advice on how to prepare for the test can be found at www.mpw.co.uk/getintomed.

The test is sat at a test centre – there are 150 test centres in the UK and many overseas. To register for the test, you need to go to the UKCAT website (www.ukcat.ac.uk). The site also contains details about the test content and practice tests. Unlike other entrance tests, UKCAT is sat before you apply. On-line registration for the test starts in early June, and the last sittings are in mid-October, a few days before the deadline for medical applications.

The medical schools use the test scores in different ways. Some will specify a minimum mark, others will call the only top scorers for interview, whilst others will use the score alongside all of the other entrance criteria as an extra piece of evidence.

COMMITMENT   **HAVE YOU SHOWN A GENUINE INTEREST IN MEDICINE?** This question has to be answered partly by your reference and partly by you in your personal statement but, before we go on, it's time for a bit of soul-searching in the form of a short test, shown overleaf. Get a piece of paper and do this immediately, before you read on.

THE *GETTING INTO MEDICAL SCHOOL* GENUINE INTEREST TEST

Answer all the questions, truthfully.

- ☐ Do you regularly read the following for articles about medicine?
    - ☐ Daily broadsheet newspapers
    - ☐ *New Scientist*
    - ☐ *Student BMJ*
    - ☐ www.bbc.co.uk
- ☐ Do you regularly watch *Casualty*, *Holby City*, *Doctors*, *ER*, *House* or *Grey's Anatomy*, medical documentaries such as *City Hospital* or *Street Doctors*, and current affairs programmes like *Panorama* or *Newsnight*?
- ☐ Do you possess any books or CD-ROMs about the human body or medicine, or do you visit medical websites?
- ☐ Have you attended a first-aid course?
- ☐ Have you arranged a visit to your local GP?
- ☐ Have you arranged to visit your local hospital in order to see the work of doctors at first hand?
- ☐ What day of the week does your favourite newspaper publish a health section?
- ☐ Do you know the main causes of death in this country?
- ☐ Do you know what the following stand for?
    - ☐ GMC
    - ☐ BMA
    - ☐ NICE
    - ☐ AIDS
    - ☐ SARS
    - ☐ MMR
    - ☐ MRSA
    - ☐ H5N1

MARKING THE TEST

You should have answered 'yes' to most of the first six questions and have been able to give answers to the last three. A low score (mainly 'No' and 'Don't know' answers) should make you ask yourself whether you really are sufficiently interested in medicine as a career. If you achieved a high score, you need to ensure that you communicate your interest in your UCAS application. The next paragraphs explain how, but first a note about work experience and courses.

HAVE YOU DONE RELEVANT WORK EXPERIENCE AND COURSES?

In addition to making brief visits to your local hospital and GP's surgery (which you should be able to arrange through your school or with the help of your parents), it is important to undertake a longer period of relevant work experience. If possible, try to get work experience that involves the gritty, unglamorous side of patient care. A week spent helping elderly and confused patients walk to the toilet is worth a month in the hospital laboratory helping the technicians to carry out routine tests. Unfortunately, these hospital jobs are hard to get and you may have to offer to work at weekends or at night. If that fails, you should try your local hospice or old people's home.

Hospices tend to be short of money because they are maintained by voluntary donations. They are usually happy to take on conscientious volunteers and the work they do (caring for the terminally ill) is particularly appropriate. Remember that you are not only working in a hospital/hospice in order to learn about medicine in action. You are also there to prove (to yourself as well as to the admissions tutors) that you have the dedication and stomach for what is often an unpleasant and upsetting work environment. You should be able to get the address of your nearest hospice from your GP's surgery or online.

Because of health and safety regulations, it is not always possible to arrange work experience or voluntary work with GPs, in hospitals or in hospices. The medical schools' selectors are aware of this but they will expect you to have found alternatives.

Volunteer work with a local charity is a good way of demonstrating your commitment as well as giving you the opportunity to find out more about medicine. HIV/AIDS charities, for example, welcome volunteers. A spokesman for Positive East, the leading HIV/AIDS charity in East London, says: 'Volunteers play an essential role in delivering services, providing project support, raising essential funds and are central to the charity's operation. Volunteer roles are tailored to match individual needs and full training and support is provided. Research and work placements are also available.' Contact details for Positive East can be found at the end of this book.

Any medical contact is better than none, and so clerical work in a medical environment, work in a hospital magazine stall or voluntary work for a charity working in a medical-related area is better than no work experience at all.

When you come to write the personal statement section of your UCAS application you will want to describe your practical experience of medicine in some detail. Say what you did, what you saw and what insights you gained from it. As always, include details that could provide the signpost to an interesting question in your interview. For example, suppose you write:

During the year that I worked on Sunday evenings at St Sebastian's Hospice, I saw a number of patients who were suffering from cancer and it was interesting to observe the treatment they received and watch its effects.

A generous interviewer will ask you about the management of cancer and you have an opportunity to impress if you can explain the use of drugs, radiotherapy, diet, exercise and so on.

The other benefit of work in a medical environment is that you may be able to make a good impression on the senior staff you have worked for. If they are prepared to write a brief reference and send it to your school, the teacher writing your reference will be able to quote from it.

ALWAYS KEEP A DIARY

During your work experience, keep a diary and write down what you see being done. At the time, you may think that you will remember what you saw, but there could be as long as 18 months between the work experience and an interview, and you will almost certainly forget vital details. Very often, applicants are asked at interview to expand on something interesting on their UCAS application. For example:

Interviewer: *I see that you observed a coronary angioplasty. What does that involve?*

Candidate: *Er.*

Interviewer: *Well, I know it's hard to see what's happening but I'm sure you understand the reason for carrying out a coronary angioplasty.*

Candidate: *Um.*

Don't allow this to happen to you!

The only problem with work experience is that it can be hard to persuade members of a busy medical team to spend time explaining in detail what they are doing and why. MPW and a number of other organisations (see page 103) run courses for sixth-formers to help them understand the common areas of medicine and to link this theoretical knowledge to practical procedures.

HAVE YOU BEEN INVOLVED IN YOUR LOCAL COMMUNITY?

A career in medicine involves serving the community and you need to demonstrate that you have something of the dedication needed to be a good doctor. You may have been able to do this through voluntary jobs in hospitals or hospices. If not, you need to think about devoting a regular period each week to one of the charitable organisations that cares for those in need.

The number needing this help has increased following the government's decision to close some of the long-stay mental institutions and place the burden of caring for patients on local authorities. Your local social services department (address in the phone book) will be able to give you information on this and other opportunities for voluntary work. Again, it is helpful to obtain brief references from the people you work for so that these can be included in what your teacher writes about you.

PERSONAL QUALITIES

HAVE YOU DEMONSTRATED A RANGE OF INTERESTS?
Medical schools like to see applicants who have done more with their life than work for their A levels and watch TV. While the teacher writing your reference will probably refer to your outstanding achievements in his or her reference, you also need to say something about them in your personal statement. Selectors like to read about achievements in sport and other outdoor activities such as The Duke of Edinburgh's Award Scheme. Equally useful activities include Young Enterprise, charity work, public speaking, part-time jobs, art, music and drama.

Bear in mind that selectors will be asking themselves, 'Would this person be an asset to the medical school?' Put in enough detail and try to make it interesting to read.

Here is an example of a good paragraph on interests for the personal statement section:

I very much enjoy tennis and play in the school team and for Hampshire at under-18 level. This summer a local sports shop has sponsored me to attend a tennis camp in California. I worked at the Wimbledon championships in 2006.

I have been playing the piano since the age of eight and took my Grade 7 exam recently. At school, I play in the orchestra and in a very informal jazz band. Last year I started learning the trombone but I would not like anyone except my teacher to hear my playing!

I like dancing and social events but my main form of relaxation is gardening. I have started a small business helping my neighbours to improve their gardens — which also brings in some extra money!

And here's how not to do it:

I play tennis in competitions and the piano and trombone. I like gardening.

But what if you aren't musical, can't play tennis and find geraniums boring? It depends when you are reading this. Anyone with enough drive to become a doctor can probably rustle up an interest or two in six months. If you haven't even got that long, then it would be sensible to devote most of your personal statement to your interest in medicine.

DIRE WARNINGS

1| Don't copy any of the paragraphs above slavishly on to your own UCAS application.
2| Don't write anything that isn't true.
3| Don't write anything you can't talk about at the interview.
4| Avoid over-complicated, over-formal styles of writing. Read your personal statement out loud: if it doesn't sound like you speaking, rewrite it.

HAVE YOU CONTRIBUTED TO SCHOOL ACTIVITIES?

This is largely covered by the section on interests but it is worth noting that the selector is looking for someone who will contribute to the communal life of the medical school. If you have been involved in organising things in your school, do remember to include the details. If it's true, don't forget to say that you ran the school's fundraising barbecue or that you organised a sponsored jog in aid of disabled children. Conversely, medical schools are less interested in applicants whose activities are exclusively solitary or which cannot take place in the medical school environment. Don't expect to get much credit for:

> *My main interest is going for long walks in desolate places by myself or in the company of my MP3 player.*

HAVE YOU ANY ACHIEVEMENTS OR LEADERSHIP EXPERIENCE TO YOUR CREDIT?

Again, the main points have been covered already, but you should recall that the selectors are looking for applicants who stand out and who have done more with their lives than the absolute minimum. They are particularly attracted by excellence in any sphere. Have you competed in any activity at a high level or received a prize or other recognition for your achievements? Have you organised and led any events or team games? Were you elected as class representative to the school council? If so, make sure that you include it in your personal statement.

TO WHAT EXTENT DOES YOUR REFEREE SUPPORT YOUR APPLICATION?

The vital importance of judicious grovelling to your referee and making sure that he or she knows all the good news about your work in hospitals and in the local community has already been explained. Remember that the teacher writing your reference will rely heavily on advice from other teachers too. They also need to be buttered up and helped to see you as a natural doctor. Come to school scrupulously clean and tidy. Work hard, look keen and make sure you talk about medicine in class. Ask intelligent, medicine-related questions such as the following:

Is it because enzymes become denatured at over 45°C that patients suffering from heat stroke have to be cooled down quickly using ice?

Could sex-linked diseases such as muscular dystrophy be avoided by screening the sperm to eliminate those containing the X chromosomes which carry the harmful recessive genes from an affected male?

Your friends may find all this nauseating – ignore them. They'll be laughing on the other side of their faces when you're a doctor and they are still filling supermarket shelves.

If your referee is approachable you should be able to ask whether or not he or she feels able to support your application. In the unlikely case that he or she cannot recommend you, you should consider asking if another teacher could complete the application: clashes of personality do very occasionally occur and you must not let the medical schools receive an application form which damns you.

MECHANICS OF THE UCAS APPLICATION

You will receive advice from your school and you may also find it helpful to consult the MPW guide *How to Complete Your UCAS Application* (see page 105). Some additional points that apply chiefly to medicine are set out below.

PRESENTATION

The vast majority of applications are now completed electronically through the UCAS website using the *Apply* system. The online system has many useful built-in safety checks to ensure that you do not make mistakes.

Despite the help that the electronic version provides, it is still possible to create an unfavourable impression on the selectors through spelling mistakes, grammatical errors and unclear personal statements. In order to ensure that this does not happen, follow these tips:

- Read the instructions for each section of the application carefully before filling it in.
- Double-check all dates (when you joined and left schools, when you sat examinations), examination boards, GCSE grades and personal details (fee codes, residential status codes, disability codes).
- Plan your personal statement as you would an essay. Lay it out in a logical order. Make the sentences short and to the point. Split the section into paragraphs, with headings such as 'work experience', 'reasons for choice', 'interests' and 'achievements'. This will enable the selector to read and assess it quickly and easily.
- Ask your parents, or someone who is roughly the same age as the selectors (over 30), to cast a critical eye over your draft and don't be too proud to make changes in the light of their advice.

If you do use a paper form, try to word-process the personal statement rather than handwrite it. The form is photocopied by UCAS and reduced to two-thirds of its original size. If you try to cram in too much or if your writing is difficult to decipher, the result will be illegible and the selectors will not bother to read it.

TIMING

The UCAS period is from 1 September to 15 January, but medical applications have to be with UCAS by 15

October. Late applications are also permitted, although the medical schools are not bound to consider them. Remember that most referees take at least a week to consult the relevant teachers and compile a reference, so allow for that and aim to submit your application by 1 September unless there is a good reason for delaying.

The only convincing reason for delaying is that your teachers cannot predict high A level grades at the moment but might be able to do so if they see high-quality work during the autumn term. If you are not on track for AAB/ABB by October, you still need to submit your application because, without an entry in the UCAS system, you cannot participate in Clearing (see page 60).

> **TIP:** Keep a copy of your personal statement so that you can look at it when you prepare for the interview.

WHAT HAPPENS NEXT AND WHAT TO DO ABOUT IT

Once your reference has been submitted, a receipt will be sent to your school or college to acknowledge its arrival. Your application is then processed and UCAS will send you confirmation of your details. If you don't receive this you should check with your referee that it has been correctly submitted. It will contain your application number, your details and the list of courses you have applied to. Check carefully to make sure that the details in your application have been saved to the UCAS system correctly. At the same time make a note of your UCAS number – you will need to quote this when you contact the medical schools.

Now comes a period of waiting which can be very unsettling but which must not be allowed to distract you from your work. Most medical schools decide whether or not they want to interview you within a month but there are some categories, such as retake students, who will not be called for interview until the new year; in some cases, the medical school may wait until March, when the results of any January retake exams are known.

If you have applied to one of those medical schools which do not interview A level candidates, the next communication you receive may be a notification from UCAS that you have been made a conditional offer.

If one or more of the medical schools decides to interview you, your next letter will be an invitation to visit the school and attend an interview. (For advice on how to prepare for the interview see Chapter 2.)

If you are unlucky, the next correspondence you get from UCAS will contain the news that you have been rejected by one or more of your choices. Does that mean it's time to relax on the A level work and dust off alternative plans? Should you be reading up on exactly what the four-year course in 'Road Resurfacing' involves? No, you should not! A rejection is a setback and it does make the path into medicine that bit steeper, but it isn't an excuse to give up.

A rejection should act as a spur to work even harder because the grades you achieve at A level are now even more important. Don't give up and do turn to page 59 to see what to do when you get your A level results.

2

GETTING AN OFFER

The idea of preparing for an interview is a
relatively new one, and there are still many
people who feel that you can't (or shouldn't) do
so. Nevertheless, there is a fundamental weak-
ness in the theory that the panel will somehow
dismiss what you say and how you look as they
unerringly uncover the 'real you'. Wise and expe-
rienced though the interviewers may be, they do
not have the ability to examine the deep recesses
of the soul. They cannot ignore the words you
didn't mean to say or supply the ones you left
out.

Success in an interview, like success in any other human
activity, depends on preparation and practice. The first
time you try to do something you usually get it wrong, if
only because unfamiliarity leads to nervousness. Practice
is particularly important because the medical schools
rarely give a second chance to someone who makes a bad
impression at interview.

To help you practise, this chapter lists many typical questions and includes discussion of how to answer them.

There is a section on how you can take charge of the interview and encourage the interviewers to ask you the questions you want to answer. There is a list of sample questions for a mock interview and, finally, there is a brief explanation of what will happen after your interviews.

The questions included here are real questions that have been put to applicants over the last two years. They have been gleaned from students who have faced interviews, from admissions tutors and through sitting in on the real thing. As explained later, you cannot prepare for the odd, unpredictable questions – but the interviewers are not trying to catch you out and they can be relied on to ask some of the general questions that are discussed here.

For many questions there are no 'right' answers and, even if there were, you shouldn't trot them out parrot fashion. The purpose of presenting the questions, and some strategies for answering them, is to help you think about your answers before the interview and to enable you to put forward your own views clearly and with confidence.

When you have read through this section, and thought about the questions, arrange for someone to sit down with you and take you through the mock interview questions on page 53. (If you have the facilities, you will find it helpful to record the interview on video, for later analysis.) You might be interested in the views of four medical professionals, quoted in the November 2002 edition of the *Student BMJ*, on the qualities that they look for.

Peter McCrorie, Director of the Graduate Entry Programme at St George's:

> ... an understanding about what being a good doctor entails from both the profession's point of view and the patient's point of view; a significant, meaningful experience of working in a healthcare environment or with disabled or disadvantaged people; an understanding of the importance of research in medicine; an awareness of the ethical issues associated with medical research; good oral communication skills and evidence of flexible and critical thinking.

Dr Allan Cumming, Associate Dean of Teaching at
Edinburgh University:

> The innate characteristics of a good doctor are beneficence and
> the capacity to engage with the knowledge necessary for
> informed practice.

Mike Shooter, President of the Royal College of
Psychiatrists:

> I think that you are born with some personal qualities, such as
> the ability to get on with people, to empathise with their dis-
> tress, to inspire confidence in others, and to carry anxiety. Such
> qualities are very difficult to train into a person. A good doctor
> also needs knowledge and the experience of implementing that
> knowledge.

John Tooke, Dean of the Peninsula Medical School:

> A medical student needs to be bright – not least to cope with a
> lifetime of assimilation of new concepts and knowledge. The
> ability to communicate, the ability to work as part of a multi-
> professional team, empathy and a non-prejudicial approach are
> qualities that should be expected in all healthcare profession-
> als. There is also, however, a need for diversity and a need to
> resist any move towards personality conformity.

Finally, don't forget that medical school interviewers are
busy people and they do not interview for the fun of it.
Neither do they set out to humiliate you. They call you
for interview because they want to offer you a place –
make it easy for them to do so!

**TYPICAL
INTERVIEW
QUESTIONS
AND HOW TO
HANDLE THEM**

QUESTIONS DESIGNED TO TEST MOTIVATION

WHY DO YOU WANT TO BECOME A DOCTOR?
The question that most interviewees dread! Answers that
will turn your interviewers' stomachs and may lead to
rejection are:

> I want to heal sick people.

> My father is a doctor and I want to be like him.

The money's good and unemployment among doctors is low.

The careers teacher told me to apply.

It's glamorous.

I want to join a respected profession, so it is either this or Law.

Try the question now. Most sixth-formers find it quite hard to give an answer and are often not sure why they want to be a doctor. Often the reasons are lost in the mists of time and have simply been reinforced over the years.

The interviewers will be sympathetic but they do require an answer that sounds convincing. There are four general strategies:

The story (option A)
You tell the interesting (and true) story of how you have always been interested in medicine, how you have made an effort to find out what is involved by visiting your local hospital, working with your GP, etc, and how this long-term and deep-seated interest has now become something of a passion. (Stand by for searching questions designed to check that you know what you are talking about!)

The story (option B)
You tell the interesting (and true) story of how you, or a close relative, suffered from an illness which brought you into contact with the medical profession. This experience made you think of becoming a doctor and, since then, you have made an effort to find out what is involved... (as before).

The logical elimination of alternatives
In this approach you have analysed your career options and decided that you want to spend your life in a scientific environment (you have enjoyed science at school) but would find pure research too impersonal. Therefore the idea of a career that combines the excitement of scientific investigation with a great deal of human contact is attractive. Since discovering that medicine offers this combination you have investigated it (and other alterna-

tives) thoroughly (visits to hospitals, GPs, etc) and have become passionately committed to your decision.

The problems with this approach are that:

- They will have heard it all before.
- You will find it harder to convince them of your passion for medicine.

Fascination with people

Some applicants can honestly claim to have a real interest in people. Here's a test to see if you are one of them:

You are waiting in the queue for a bus/train/supermarket checkout. Do you ignore the other people in the queue or do you start chatting to them? Win extra points if they spontaneously start chatting to you and a bonus if, within five minutes, they have told you their life story. Applicants with this seemingly magical power to empathise with their fellow human beings do, if they have a matching interest in human biology, have a good claim to a place at medical school.

Whether you choose one of these strategies or one of your own, your answer must be well-considered and convincing. Additionally, it should sound natural and not over-rehearsed. Bear in mind that most of your interviewers will be doctors, and they (hopefully) will have chosen medicine because they, like you, had a burning desire to do so. They will not expect you to be able to justify your choice by reasoned argument alone. Statements (as long as they are supported by evidence of practical research) such as '... *and the more work I did at St James's, the more I realised that medicine is what I desperately want to do...*' are quite acceptable – and far more convincing than saying '*Medicine is the only career that combines science and the chance to work with people*', because it isn't!

WHAT HAVE YOU DONE TO SHOW YOUR COMMITMENT TO MEDICINE AND TO THE COMMUNITY?

This should tie in with your UCAS application. Your answer should demonstrate that you do have a genuine interest in helping others. Ideally, you will have a track record of regular visits to your local hospital or hospice where you will have worked in the less attractive side of patient care (such as cleaning bedpans). Acceptable alternatives are regular visits to an elderly person to do their chores, or work with one of the charities that care for the homeless or other disadvantaged groups.

It isn't sufficient to have worked in a laboratory, out of sight of patients, or to have done so little work as to be trivial. (*'I once walked around the ward of the local hospital – it was very nice.'*)

You may find that an answer such as this leads the interviewer to ask: *'If you enjoyed working in the hospital so much, why don't you want to become a nurse?'* This is a tough question. You need to indicate that, while you admire enormously the work that nurses do, you would like the challenge of diagnosis and of deciding what treatment should be given.

WHY HAVE YOU APPLIED TO THIS MEDICAL SCHOOL?
Don't say:

It's well equipped.

I like the buildings.

It's easy to get into.

My dad's the Dean.

It has a good reputation (unless you know exactly what for).

Some of the reasons that you might have are:

■ **Thorough investigation:** You have made a thorough investigation of a number of the medical schools that you have considered. You have been to an open day and talked to current medical students. You have spoken to the admissions tutor about your particular situation and asked their advice about suitable work experience, and he or she was particularly encouraging and helpful. You feel that the general atmosphere is one you would love to be part of.

- **Course structure:** You have read the prospectus (don't forget to) and feel that the course is structured in an interesting way. You like the fact that it is integrated and that students are brought into contact with patients at an early date. Another related reason might be that you are attracted by the subject-based or system-based teaching approach. A subject-based course covers the material in terms of academic subjects like biochemistry or anatomy whereas a systems-based course looks at the body's systems (eg the cardiovascular system).
- **Recommendation from teacher:** Your careers teacher at school recommended the school. Careers teachers make it their business to find out about individual medical schools and they will also receive feedback from their former pupils. An informed recommendation is a perfectly valid reason for choosing a particular medical school. The same applies to advice you may read in this or other books.
- **Recommendation from friend:** A variation on the careers teacher theme: you may have a recommendation from your own personal friends or informed friends of your parents. In this case you must be able to quote the names of these friends.

Don't forget that all the UK medical schools and university departments of medicine are well equipped and offer a high standard of teaching. It is therefore perfectly reasonable to say that, while you have no specific preference at this stage, you do have a great deal to give to any school that offers you a place. This answer will, inevitably, lead on to *'Well, tell us what you do have to give?'* That question is discussed on page 48.

QUESTIONS DESIGNED TO ASSESS YOUR KNOWLEDGE OF MEDICINE

No one expects you to know all about your future career before you start at medical school, but they do expect you to have made an effort to find out something about it. If you are really interested in medicine, you will have a reasonable idea of common illnesses and diseases, and you will be aware of topical issues. Remember the genuine interest test on page 16. The questions aimed at testing your knowledge of medicine divide into six main areas:

- The human body (and what can go wrong with it)
- The medical profession
- The National Health Service – funding health
- Private medicine
- Ethical questions
- Other issues

THE HUMAN BODY (AND WHAT CAN GO WRONG WITH IT)
The interviewers will expect you to be interested in medicine and to be aware of current problems and new treatments. In both cases the list is endless but the following are some areas with which you should familiarise yourself.

Your personal area of interest
This is how the questions might go:

Interviewer:	*You have written on your UCAS application that you are interested in how the human body works. Which system particularly interests you?*
Candidate:	*Um, the brain.*
Interviewer:	*Tell us how the brain works.*
Candidate:	*Um, oh dear. I'm very sorry, I've forgotten.*
Interviewer:	(with pleasure as they spring the trap) *Well, that's a real pity because there are only two people in the world who know how the brain works. One is God and he won't tell us and the other is you and you've forgotten.* (Laughs all round at your expense)

Avoid this trap by choosing, in advance, a relatively well-understood body system such as the cardiovascular system, then learn how it works and (particularly for interviews at Oxbridge) prepare for fundamental questions like *'What is meant by myocardial infarction?'* and questions about what can go wrong with the system – see below.

Your own work experience
If you are able to arrange work experience in a medical environment you will want to include it in your personal

statement; but make sure that you keep a diary and that you enter in it not only what you saw, but also medical details of what was happening. For example, note not only that a patient was brought into casualty but what the symptoms were, what the diagnosis was and what treatment was given.

Here is an example of a bad answer:

Interviewer: *I notice that you spent two weeks at St James's. Tell me something about what you did there.*
Candidate: *I spent two days in the Cardiology department, three days in A&E, one day in the Pathology lab, two days on an Oncology ward, one and a half days in Neurology and half a day in General Surgical. I saw sutures, drips, lung cancer... [etc]*

The problem here is that the interviewers are no clearer about your suitability for a career in medicine, only that you have a good memory. This approach is referred to by some admissions tutors as *medical tourism*.

> **TIP:** Interviewers are looking for a genuine enthusiasm for medicine. They are not going to be impressed by a long list of hospital departments, treatments or illnesses unless they can see that your experience actually meant something to you on a personal level, and that you gained insights into the profession.

Here is a better answer:

I was able to spend time in a number of wards, which enabled me to see a whole range of treatments. For instance, during my two days in the Cardiology department, I was able to see several newly admitted patients who might have had heart attacks. I found it particularly interesting to see how careful the doctors had to be in taking the history, so that they were not putting words into the patients' mouths about their symptoms and the type of pain they were experiencing. I was also able to watch an angioplasty being performed. I was amazed at the level of skill the surgeon demonstrated — I would love to do that myself one day.

In this type of answer, your genuine enthusiasm, good observation and respect for the profession are all apparent.

Keeping a file of cuttings

Make sure that you read *New Scientist*, *Student BMJ* and, on a daily basis, a broadsheet newspaper which carries regular, high-quality medical reporting. The *Independent* has excellent coverage of current health issues, and the *Guardian*'s health section on Tuesdays is informative and interesting. Newspapers' websites often group articles thematically which can save time. The Sunday broadsheets often contain comprehensive summaries of the week's top medical stories.

The big killers

Diseases affecting the circulation of the blood (including heart disease) and cancer are the main causes of death in the UK. Make sure you know the factors that contribute towards them and the strategies for prevention and treatment. Their importance is illustrated by the following table, giving mortality rates in the UK for 2005.

Cause of death	Male	Female
All	243,324	269,368
Infectious diseases	2,664	3,477
Ischaemic heart disease	49,317	38,954
Respiratory disease	32,689	39,828
Cancer – all	71,878	66,576
Cancer – respiratory system	17,524	12,180
Cancer – digestive system	20,935	16,720
Cancer – breast	81	11,040
Cancer – secondary	5,530	6,482
Cancer – colon	4,587	4,489
Cancer – prostate	9,042	0
Cancer – skin	1,120	955

Source: www.statistics.gov.uk

You should be able to discuss possible reasons for the changes in death rates from causes such as cancer and heart problems, and for the difference in mortality rates between men and women.

The global picture

The world population is about 6.2 billion, and growing. Last year, around 60 million people died. The biggest killers are infectious diseases (11 million) such as AIDS, malaria and tuberculosis, and circulatory diseases (17 million) such as coronary heart disease and stroke. Cancer killed about 7 million people.

Infectious diseases that were once thought to be under control, such as tuberculosis, cholera and yellow fever, have made a comeback. This is due, in part, to the increasing resistance of certain bacteria to antibiotics. The antibiotics that we use now are essentially modifications to drugs that have been in use for the last 30 or 40 years, and random genetic mutations allow resistant strains to multiply. Current Issues (page 79) gives more background information, including an assessment of the differences between developed and developing countries' health issues.

The effects of an ageing population

Life expectancy continues to rise (except in many sub-Saharan African countries which have been ravaged by HIV/AIDS – see page 98) because of improvements in sanitation and medical care. According to the World Health Organization (WHO), the number of people aged sixty or over will more than triple by 2050, from about 600 million now, to 2 billion. Birth rates in most countries are falling, and the combination of the two brings considerable problems. The relative numbers of people who succumb to chronic illness (such as cancer, diabetes or diseases of the circulatory system) is increasing and this puts greater strains on countries' healthcare systems. A useful indicator is the Dependency Ratio – the percentage of the population that is economically dependent on the active age group. It is calculated as the sum of 0- to 14-year-olds and over-65s divided by the number of people aged between 15 and 59. This is rising steadily. The WHO website contains data for each country – its address can be found at the end of the book.

The Human Genome Project and gene therapy

Arguably, the most important scientific work of the last century was the discovery of the structure of DNA and the identification of the human genes. The Human Genome Project, the mapping of all human genes, made great progress during the 1990s and many of the illnesses that have their origins in genetic defects were identified. The defective genes have been listed and tests developed to enable the individuals who carry them to be made aware of the fact. This in itself raises some ethical and moral issues.

You would be wise to familiarise yourself with the sequence of developments in the field of genetic research, starting with the discovery of the double helix structure of DNA by Crick and Watson in 1953. You should find out all that you can about:

- Recombinant DNA technology (gene therapy, genetic engineering)
- Genetic diagnosis (of particular interest to insurance companies)
- Cloning (see page 91)
- Stem cell research
- GM crops
- Genetic enhancement of livestock
- 'Pharming'.

Fashionable illnesses

At any one time the media tend to concentrate on one or two 'fashionable' diseases. The papers fill their pages with news of the latest 'epidemic' and the general public is expected to react as if the great plague of 1665 were just round the corner. In reality, ebola, CJD and SARS resulted in very small numbers of deaths and the same can (so far) be said of the current hot topic, bird flu. The media encourage us to react emotionally rather than logically in matters concerning risk. They advise us to stop eating beef but not to stop driving our cars, even though around 3,000 people are killed in road accidents every year.

While these diseases tend to be trivial in terms of their effect, they are often interesting in scientific terms and the fact that they are being discussed in the media makes it likely that they will come up at interview. A typical question would be *'Why is bird flu causing so much concern, when very few people have died from it?'*

It is important to know something about these illnesses (see Chapter 5 and www.mpw.co.uk/getintomed for links to information on bird flu, SARS, MRSA, mad cows and CJD) but equally important to keep them in statistical proportion. For example, nearly two million people die as a result of contracting diarrhoeal infections each year, mostly the result of poor sanitation and infected water supplies, and over five million people die as a result of injury sustained in accidents or violence.

Diet, exercise and the environment

The maintenance of health on a national scale isn't simply a matter of waiting until people get ill and then rushing in with surgery or medicine to cure them. There is good evidence that illness can be prevented by sensible diet, not smoking, taking exercise and living in a healthy environment. In this context, a healthy environment means one where food and water are uncontaminated by bacteria and living quarters are well ventilated, warm and dry. The huge advance in health and life expectancy since the middle of the nineteenth century owes much more to these factors than to the achievements of modern medicine.

> **TIP:** When discussing medical topics you will sound more convincing if you learn and use the correct terminology. For example, to a doctor, a patient doesn't *turn up at the surgery with high blood pressure*; he *presents with hypertension*. The best sources of correct terminology are medical textbooks, some of which are quite easy to understand (see Chapter 6).

THE MEDICAL PROFESSION

The typical question is: *'What makes a good doctor?'* Avoid answering: *'A caring and sympathetic nature.'* If these really were the crucial qualities of a good doctor there would be little point in going to medical school. Start by stressing the importance of the aspects that can be taught and, in particular, emphasise the technical qualities that a doctor needs: the ability to carry out a thorough examination, to diagnose accurately and quickly what is wrong and the skill to choose and organise the correct treatment.

After this comes the ability to communicate effectively and sympathetically with the patient so that he or she can understand and participate in the treatment. The most important part of communication is listening. There is an old medical adage that if you listen to the patient for long enough he or she will give you the diagnosis.

Communication skills also have an important role to play in treatment – studies have shown that some patients get better more quickly when they feel involved and part of the medical team. If you want, you can conclude with: *'Good personal organisation and stamina for the infamous 80-hour week.'*

THE NATIONAL HEALTH SERVICE – FUNDING HEALTH
An application to a medical school is also an application for a job and you should have taken the trouble to find out something about your likely future employer. The questions *'Is there anything wrong with the NHS?'* and *'What would you do if you were the Secretary of State for Health?'* are tricky. Your first move should be to recognise and state that the core of the NHS consists, for the most part, of highly dedicated people working extremely hard and that the vast majority of patients speak very highly of the treatment they have received.

So what is wrong? The main problems of the NHS centre on the long waiting lists for treatment and the long hours worked by doctors. In the end, both come down to money – or the lack of it. The Conservative government believed that the old, pre-1992 structure of the service did not allow efficient use of resources, hence its reforms of which you must be aware. These reforms were unpopular with some sections of the medical profession, the criticism being that they put 'profits before patients'. In December 1997, the new Labour government published a White Paper entitled *The New NHS: Modern, Dependable*. A summary of the various reforms and the developments that followed is given in Chapter 5.

Consider this line of questioning:

Interviewer: *If you were in charge, would you spend more money on the NHS?*

Candidate: *Yes.*
Interviewer: *Where would you get the money from?*

It's best not to go down this path which, in essence, leads to a discussion of economics and politics rather than medicine. If you do get trapped, you should show that you know the facts. You could then list the five main sources of extra money:

1 | Higher taxes
2 | Increased use of private health insurance (another form of tax)
3 | More government borrowing
4 | Reallocation of money from other government programmes
5 | Change to the balance of spending so that less is spent on administration and more is spent on treatment.

Historically, no government has found it possible to give the NHS all the money it needs when the costs of drugs and new equipment are rising much faster than inflation. One must conclude that full funding for the NHS, which would be a great vote winner at any election, is very difficult. If the finest political and economic brains in the country have failed to find a solution, you probably won't either.

PRIVATE MEDICINE
Another set of questions that needs careful thought concerns private medicine. Don't forget that many consultants have flourishing private practices and rely on private work for a major part of their income. Equally, a number of doctors do not have the opportunity to practise privately and may resent a system that allows some consultants to earn money both within and outside the NHS.

Your best bet is to look at the philosophy behind private medicine and you may care to argue as follows:

> *Most people agree that if you are run over by a bus you should be taken to hospital and treated at the taxpayers' expense. In general, urgent treatment for serious and life-threatening*

conditions should be treated by the NHS and we should all chip in to pay for it. On the other hand, most of us would agree that someone who doesn't particularly care for the shape of his nose and who wants to change it by expensive plastic surgery should pay for the operation himself. We can't ban cosmetic operations so we are led to accept the right of private medicine to exist.

Having established these two extremes, one is left to argue about the point where the two systems meet. Should there be a firm dividing line or a fuzzy one where both the NHS and private medicine operate? Currently the line is fuzzy.

You could also point out that private medicine should not harm the NHS. For example, the NHS has a problem of waiting lists. If ten people are standing in a queue for a bus, everyone benefits if four of those waiting jump into a taxi – providing, of course, that they don't persuade the bus driver to drive it!

Now try this question yourself: *'Is it fair that a rich person should be able to buy better health than a poor person?'* (Hint: start by examining the assumption made in the question.)

TIP: This question illustrates an effective general technique for answering difficult moral, ethical or legal questions. The interviewers are not particularly interested in your opinion, but they are interested in whether you have understood the issues. Always demonstrate this by explaining the extreme opposing views. Only then, and in a balanced and reasonable way, give your own opinion.

ETHICAL QUESTIONS

Medical ethics is a fascinating area of moral philosophy. You won't be expected to answer questions on the finer points but you could be asked about the issues below.

You should remember that the interviewers are not interested in your opinions, but they are interested in whether you have understood the issues. A useful approach to this type of question is:

1 | Explain the background to the question(s).
2 | Consider both sides of the argument.

3 | Bring current issues or examples into your answer.
4 | Only express a personal opinion at the very end.

A patient who refuses treatment

You could be presented with a scenario, and asked what you would do in the situation. For example, you have to inform a patient that he has cancer. Without radiotherapy and chemotherapy his life expectancy is likely to be a matter of months. The patient tells you that he does not wish to be treated. Two months later, the patient dies and shortly afterwards you are confronted by his wife who accuses you of ruining her life and that of her five-year-old daughter.

- What would you have done when the patient told you that he did not want to receive treatment?
- How would you have responded to the wife's accusations?

The first thing to remember is that the interviewer is not asking you this question because he or she wants to know what the answer to this problem is. Questions of this nature are designed to see whether you can look at problems from different angles, weigh up arguments, use your knowledge of medical issues to come to a conclusion, and produce coherent and structured answers.

A possible starting point for your answer to this question could be:

> First of all, a doctor cannot force a patient to undergo treatment. As long as, in your judgement, the patient is capable of making rational decisions, he is entitled to take your advice and then disregard it. In this case, the first thing I would do is to try to ascertain why the patient does not want to undergo treatment. It might be for religious or moral reasons; it might simply be that he has heard stories about the side effects of the treatment you have recommended. One possible route would be to give him contact details of a suitable support group, counselling service or information centre.

A classic case is someone who refuses a life-saving blood transfusion because it contravenes his or her religious beliefs. Fair enough, you may feel, but what if, on these grounds, a parent refuses to allow a baby's life to be saved by a transfusion? Similarly, in a well-publicised legal case, a woman refused to allow a Caesarean delivery of her baby. The judge ruled that the wishes of the mother could be overruled. It is worth noting that the NHS (as a representative of the state) has no right to keep a patient in hospital against his or her will unless the medical team and relatives use the powers of the Mental Health Act.

Euthanasia

Start by making sure that you know the following correct terminology, and the law.

- **Suicide:** The act of killing oneself intentionally.
- **Physician-assisted suicide:** This involves a doctor intentionally giving a person advice on or the means to commit suicide. It describes situations where competent people want to kill themselves but lack either the means or the ability.
- **Euthanasia:** Euthanasia is a deliberate act or omission whose primary intention is to end another's life. Literally, it means a gentle or easy death but has come to signify a deliberate intervention with the intention to kill someone, often described as the 'mercy killing' of people in pain with terminal illnesses.
- **Double effect:** The principle of double effect provides the justification for the provision of medical treatment which has a negative effect although the intention is to provide an overall positive effect. The principle permits an act which foreseeably has both good and bad effects, provided that the good effect is the reason for acting and is not caused by the bad. A common example is the provision of essential pain-relieving drugs in terminal care, at the risk of shortening life. Pain relief is the intention and outweighs the risks of shortening life.
- **Non-treatment:** Competent adults have the right to refuse any treatment, including life-prolonging procedures. The BMA does not consider valid treatment refusal by a patient to be suicide. Respecting a competent, informed patient's treatment refusal is not assisting suicide.

■ **Withdrawing/withholding life-prolonging medical treatment:** Not all treatment with the potential to prolong life has to be provided in all circumstances, especially if its effect is seen as extending the dying process. Cardio-pulmonary resuscitation of a terminally ill cancer patient is an extreme example. In deciding which treatment should be offered, the expectation must be that the advantages outweigh the drawbacks for the individual patient.

Euthanasia is illegal in the United Kingdom, and doctors who are alleged to have given a patient a lethal dose of a medication with the intention of ending that person's life have been charged with murder. UK law also prohibits assisting with suicide. The Suicide Act 1961 decriminalised suicide in England and Wales, but assisting a suicide is a crime under that legislation. The Act states that:

> A person who aids, abets, counsels or procures the suicide of another, or an attempt by another to commit suicide, shall be liable on conviction on indictment to imprisonment for a term not exceeding fourteen years ...

> If on the trial of an indictment for murder or manslaughter it is proved that the accused aided, abetted, counselled or procured the suicide of the person in question, the jury may find them guilty of that offence.

In December 2004, a High Court judge allowed a husband to take his wife (referred to as Mrs Z in the case) to Switzerland, where the law on euthanasia is different, to help her to die. Mrs Z was unable to travel alone as she had an incurable brain disease, but the local authorities had tried to prevent her husband taking her. It is now expected that more people in the UK will travel to Switzerland to be allowed to die. It was reported in the *Observer* in December 2004 that an estimated 3% of GPs in the UK had helped patients to die. The *Observer* also stated that in a poll of doctors, 54% favoured legalising euthanasia. The BMA website provides detailed information on the law in a number of countries, and the ethical considerations behind euthanasia. Links to this, and to other related websites, can be found on www.mpw.co.uk/getintomed.

So one of the key questions is *'Could you withdraw treatment from a patient for whom the prognosis was very poor, who seemed to enjoy no quality of life and who was in great pain?'*

The answer to this question comes in two parts. First, you must recognise that a decision like this could not be taken without the benefit of full medical training and some experience, together with the advice of colleagues and the fullest consultation with the patient and his or her relations. If, after that process, it was clear that life support should be withdrawn, then, and only then, would you take your decision. Part two involves convincing the panel that, having taken your decision, you would act on it.

Difficult choices – who should be treated at public expense?

A good opening question is *'Should smokers be treated on the NHS?'* On the one hand, it is certainly true that smoking is a contributory factor in heart disease. Is it fair to expect the community as a whole to spend a great deal of money on, for example, coronary artery bypass surgery if the patient refuses to abandon behaviour that could jeopardise the long-term effectiveness of the operation? Conversely, one can argue that all citizens and certainly all taxpayers have the right to treatment irrespective of their lifestyles. Further to this, one can argue that duty paid on cigarettes adds up to more than the cost of treatment.

Another series of questions recognises the fact that there is a limit to the resources available to the NHS and highlights the tough decisions that may need to be taken. The interviewer might refer to 'rationing of healthcare'. Suppose you have resources for one operation but two critically ill patients – how do you decide which one to save? Or, suppose that you can perform six hip replacement operations for the cost of one coronary artery bypass. Heart bypass operations save life; hip replacements merely improve it. Which option should you go for?

Even more controversial issues surround surgery to change gender. Should these operations be performed when the money could be used to save, or at least to prolong, life?

OTHER ISSUES

Events are constantly bringing fresh moral issues associated with medicine into the public arena. It is important that you read the papers and maintain an awareness of the current 'hot' issues. See Chapter 6 for further reading.

QUESTIONS AIMED AT FINDING OUT WHETHER YOU WILL FIT IN

One of the reasons for interviewing you is to see whether you will fit successfully into both the medical school and the medical profession. The interviewers will try to find out if your views and approach to life are likely to make you an acceptable colleague in a profession which, to a great extent, depends on teamwork. This does not mean that they want to hear views identical to their own. On the contrary, they will welcome ideas that are refreshing and interesting. What they do not like to hear is arrogance, lies, bigotry or tabloid headlines.

These questions have another important purpose: to assess your ability to communicate in a friendly and effective way with strangers even when under pressure. This skill will be very important when you come to deal with patients.

QUESTIONS ABOUT YOUR UCAS APPLICATION

The personal statement section, in which you write about yourself, is a fertile area for questions and, as explained earlier, you should have included some juicy morsels to attract the interviewers. The most successful interviews often revolve around some interesting or amusing topic that is fun to talk about and that makes you stand out from the crowd. The trouble is that you cannot invent such a topic – it really has to exist. Nevertheless, if you really have been involved in a campaign to save an obscure species of toad and can tell a couple of amusing stories about it (make them short), so much the better.

Even if your UCAS application seems, in retrospect, a bit dull, don't worry. Work out something interesting to say. Look at what you wrote and at all costs avoid the really major disasters: if you put that you like reading, for instance, make sure you can remember and talk intelligently about the last book you read.

Sometimes an amusing comment on your application followed up by a relaxed and articulate performance at the interview will do the trick. A good example is the comment that a student made about lasting only three days as a waitress during the summer holidays. She was able to tell a story about dropped food and dry-cleaning bills, and was offered a place. Of course, failing at a part-time job is only going to be a funny story if you are relaxed enough to make it amusing and you have already proved to the interviewers that you are a strong candidate for whom this incident was an anomaly.

QUESTIONS ABOUT YOUR CONTRIBUTION TO THE LIFE OF THE MEDICAL SCHOOL

These questions can come in many forms but, once identified, they need to be tackled carefully. If you say you like social life, the selectors might worry that you won't pass your pre-clinical exams. On the other hand, if you say that you plan to spend all your time windsurfing, mountaineering or fishing, they'll see you as a loner.

Probably the best approach is to say that you realise that medical school is hard work and that your main responsibility must be to pass your exams. After that, you could say that the medical school can only function as a community if the individuals involved are prepared to participate enthusiastically in as many of the extracurricular activities as possible. Above all, try to talk about communal and team activities rather than more solitary pursuits.

You may find it helpful to know that, in one London medical school, the interviewers are told to ask themselves if the candidate has made good use of the opportunities available to them, and whether they have the personal qualities and interests appropriate to student life and a subsequent career in medicine. Poor communication skills, excessive shyness or lack of enthusiasm concern them, and will be taken into account when awarding scores.

UNPREDICTABLE QUESTIONS

There are two types of unpredictable question: nice and nasty.

NICE QUESTIONS

Nice questions are usually designed to test your communication skills and to assess your personality. A typical nice question would be 'If you won a million pounds on the lottery, what would you do with it?'

Rule 1: Don't relax! Your answer to this question needs to be as effective and articulate as any other and, while you should appear to be relaxed, you must not let your thinking or speech become sloppy.

Rule 2: A nice question could also indicate that the interviewer has decided against you and simply wants to get through the allotted time as easily as possible. If you suspect that this is the case (possibly because you have said something that you now regret), this question provides an opportunity to redeem yourself. Try to steer the questions back to gritty, medically related topics. See the advice on page 52.

NASTY QUESTIONS

The 'interview nasties' are included either as a test of your reaction to pressure or in response to something you have said in answer to a previous question. Here are some examples:

Why should we give you a place here when we have many better-qualified applicants?

Don't you think that someone with the views you have just expressed would find it almost impossible to function effectively as an NHS doctor?

There are no right answers but there is a correct approach. Start by fixing the interviewer with a big smile then distance the question from your own case. Taking the first question, you could say that you realise that medical school selection is a tough business and that the criteria must be hard to define. On the one hand it must be tempting to select those whose previous work indicates that they will sail through their pre-clinical exams but, on the other, you can think of brilliant academics who find it hard to communicate. You believe that you do have something to offer the profession.

In general, the technique once again is to identify the extreme answers to the question and then, almost as an afterthought, give your own position. This approach shows the interviewers that you are capable of logical reasoning under pressure.

QUESTIONS ABOUT YOUR OWN ACADEMIC PERFORMANCE

These are especially likely if you are retaking A levels (or have retaken them). The question will be *'Why did you do so badly in your A levels?'* Don't say *'I'm thick and lazy'*, however true you feel that is!

Another bad ploy is to blame your teachers. It's part of the unspoken freemasonry of teaching that no teacher likes to hear another teacher blamed for poor results. If, however, your teacher was absent for part of the course, it is perfectly acceptable to explain this. You should also explain any other external circumstances such as illness or family problems even if you believe them to have been included in the UCAS reference. Sadly, most applicants don't have one of these cast-iron excuses!

The best answer, if you can put your hand on your heart when you deliver it, is to say that you were so involved in other school activities (head of school, captain of cricket, rowing and athletics, chairman of the Community Action Group and producer of the school play) that your work suffered. You can't really be blamed for getting the balance between work and your other activities a little bit skewed and, even if you don't have a really impressive list of other achievements, you should be able to construct an

answer on this basis. You might also add that the setback
allowed you to analyse your time-management skills, and
that you now feel you are much more effective in your
use of time.

You may also be asked how you expect to do in your A
level exams. You need to show that you are working hard,
enjoying the subjects and expect to achieve at least ABB
(or more probably AAB – check Table 2 on page 116 for
admissions policies to the different medical schools).

YOUR QUESTIONS FOR THE INTERVIEWERS

At the end of the interview the person chairing the panel
may ask if you have any questions you would like to put to
the interviewers. Bear in mind that the interviews are
carefully timed, and that your attempts to impress the
panel with 'clever' questions may do quite the opposite.
The golden rule is: only ask a question if you are genuinely interested in the answer (which, of course, you
were unable to find during your careful reading of the
prospectus and website).

QUESTIONS TO AVOID

- *What is the structure of the first year of the course?*
- *Will I be able to live in a hall of residence?*
- *When will I first have contact with patients?*
- *Can you tell me about the intercalated BSc option?*

As well as being boring questions, the answers to these
will be available in the prospectus and on the website, and
you will show that you have obviously not done any
serious research.

QUESTIONS YOU COULD ASK

- *I haven't studied Physics A level. Do you think I should go
  through some Physics textbooks before the start of the course?*
This shows that you are keen, and that you want to make
sure that you can cope with the course. It will give them a
chance to talk about the extra course they offer for non-
physicists.

■ *Do you think I should try to get more work experience before the start of the course?*

Again, an indication of your keenness.

■ *Earlier, I couldn't answer the question you asked me on why smoking causes coronary heart disease. What is the reason?*

Something that you genuinely might want to know.

■ *How soon will you let me know if I have been successful or not?*

Something you really want to know.

Remember: if in doubt, don't ask a question. End by saying *'All of my questions have been answered by the prospectus and the students who showed me around the medical school. Thank you very much for an enjoyable day.'* Big smile, shake hands and say goodbye.

HOW TO STRUCTURE THE INTERVIEW TO YOUR ADVANTAGE

Having read this far you may well be asking yourself what to do if none of the questions discussed comes up. Some of them will. Furthermore, once the interviewers have asked one of the prepared questions, you should be able to lead them on to the others. This technique is very simple and most interviewers are prepared to go along with it because it makes their job easier. All you have to do is insert a 'signpost' at the end of each answer.

Here is an example. At the end of your answer to why you want to be a doctor you could add *'I realise, of course, that medicine is moving through a period of exciting challenges and advances.'* Now stop and give the interviewer an 'over to you – I'm ready for the next question' look. Unless he or she is really trying to throw you off balance, the next question will be *'What do you know about these advances?'* Off you go with your answer but at the end you tack on *'Hand in hand with these technical changes have come changes in the administration of the NHS.'* With luck, you'll get a question about the NHS which you can answer and end with a 'signpost' to medical ethics.

You can, if you wish, plan the whole interview so that each answer leads to a new question. The last answer can be linked to the first question so as to form a loop. The interviewers have only to ask one of the questions in the loop and you are off on a pre-planned track. This idea never works perfectly, but it does enable you to maximise the amount of time you spend on prepared ground – time when, with luck, you'll be making a good impression. The disadvantage, of course, in having a set of pre-prepared answers ready is that there is a temptation to pull one out of the hat regardless of what is actually being asked. The question *'Why do you want to be a doctor?'* (which you might be expecting) requires a very different answer to the question *'Was there something that started your interest in being a doctor?'*

One final piece of advice on interviews: keep your answers relatively short and to the point. Nothing is more depressing than an answer that rambles on. If you get a question you haven't prepared, pause for thought, give them your best shot in a cheerful, positive voice and then shut up.

MOCK INTERVIEW QUESTIONS

As explained at the beginning of the chapter, interview technique can be improved with practice. You can use this section of the book as a source of mock interview questions. Your interviewer should ask supplementary questions as appropriate.

1 | Why do you want to be a doctor? (Supplementary: Are you sure you know what is involved?)
2 | (If one of your parents is a doctor.) Presumably you chose medicine because of your father or mother?
3 | What will you do if you don't get an offer from any medical schools?
4 | What evidence is there that you can cope with stress?
5 | Why have you applied to this medical school?
6 | What do you know about the course here?
7 | Have you come along to an open day here?
8 | What have you done to demonstrate your commitment to the community?
9 | What makes a good doctor?
10 | Why do you think you would make a good doctor?
11 | What did the doctors you have spoken to think about medicine as a career?

12 | What is the standard of health like in your area?

13 | Why is the standard of health more varied in London/Scotland/developing countries?

14 | Are you interested in medical research?

15 | What interests you about medicine? (Follow with questions about this area.)

16 | What do you know about AIDS? Why is it so hard to treat?

17 | What is the difference between a heart attack and a stroke?

18 | What is the link between BSE and CJD?

19 | What are the implications for doctors of an ageing population?

20 | What problems do the elderly face?

21 | What treatment can doctors offer to the very old?

22 | What do you think of homeopathy/acupuncture?

23 | How does diet affect health?

24 | How does the environment affect health?

25 | It was thought that tuberculosis (TB) had been eradicated. Why do you think that the number of TB cases is now on the increase?

26 | What roles can computers/technology play in medicine?

27 | Tell me about a recent article on medicine/science that you have read. Explain it.

28 | What are the main causes of ill health where you live?

29 | What advances in medicine can we look forward to during the next ten/twenty/fifty years ?

30 | What do you think have been the most significant developments in medicine during the last twenty/fifty/one hundred years?

31 | What is the biggest threat to humanity over the next twenty/fifty years, from a medical viewpoint?

32 | When was the NHS formed?

33 | Have the reforms of the NHS been successful?

34 | Should GPs/primary care groups act as fundholders?

35 | What do you understand by the term rationing/postcode prescribing?

36 | Do you think private practice by NHS consultants should be abolished?

37 | Who is the Secretary of State for Health? What would you do if you had to take over this role?

38 | Can anyone undertake cloning experiments in this country? What are the arguments for and against the cloning of humans?

39 | Should the UK follow Holland's example and make euthanasia legal?

40 | Is it right that the NHS should devote resources to sex-change operations when there are long waiting lists for hip replacements?

41 | Suppose that you were in charge of deciding which of two critically ill babies should have a life-saving operation. Imagine that there was not enough money to operate on both. How would you decide which baby to save?

42 | Have you come across any examples of ethical problems associated with medicine?

43 | What are your main interests? *(The interviewer must follow up the answer with searching questions.)*

44 | How do you think you will be able to contribute to the life of the medical school?

45 | What was the last book you read? Can you sum up the story in one minute?

46 | What do you do in your spare time?

47 | What is your favourite subject at A level? What do you like about it?

48 | What is your least favourite subject at A level? What do you dislike about it?

49 | *(For retake candidates or those with disappointing GCSE results)* Why did you do badly in your A levels / GCSEs?

50 | What will you do if we decide not to offer you a place here?

51 | Have you any questions for us?

POINTS FOR THE INTERVIEWER TO ASSESS

☐ Did the candidate answer in a positive, open and friendly way, maintaining eye contact for most of the time?

☐ Was the candidate's posture such that you felt that he or she was alert, friendly and enthusiastic?

☐ Was the candidate's voice pitched correctly; neither too loud nor too soft and without traces of arrogance or complacency?

☐ Was the candidate free of irritating mannerisms?
☐ Did the candidate's performance reassure you enough not to terrify you at the prospect that he or she could be your doctor in a few years?

THE PANEL

Most medical schools have so many candidates that they operate several interview panels in parallel. This means that your interview may not be chaired by the Dean but you will certainly have a senior member of the academic staff chairing the panel. He or she will normally be assisted by two or three others. Usually there are representatives of the clinical and pre-clinical staff and there may be a medical student on the board too. Sometimes a local GP is invited to join the panel. Details of the format of the interview panels can be found in Table 3 on page 118.

While you can expect the interviewers to be friendly, it is possible that one of them may use an aggressive approach. Don't be put off by this; it is a classic interview technique and will usually be balanced by a supportive member of the panel.

QUESTION-NAIRES

A number of medical schools have introduced a written component to the interview. Some, such as Nottingham and Southampton, ask for a form or an essay to be sent to them prior to the interview. Others, such as St George's and King's, give each candidate a written exercise on the day of the interview. Bear in mind that a candidate who performs well in the interview, displays the necessary academic and personal qualities, and is genuinely suited to medicine, is unlikely to be rejected on the basis of the written element.

DRESS, POSTURE AND MANNERISMS

You should dress smartly for your interview, but you should also feel comfortable. You will not be able to relax if you feel over-formal. For men, a jacket with a clean shirt and tie is ideal. Women should avoid big earrings, plunging necklines and short skirts. Men should not wear earrings, white socks or loud ties, or have (visible) piercings. They should avoid unconventional hairstyles: no mohicans or skinheads.

Your aim must be to give an impression of good personal organisation and cleanliness. Make a particular point of your hair and fingernails – you never see a doctor with dirty fingernails. Always polish your shoes before an interview, as this type of detail will be noticed. Don't go in smelling strongly of garlic, aftershave or perfume.

You will be invited to sit down, but don't fall back expansively into an armchair, cross your legs and press your fingertips together in an impersonation of Sherlock Holmes. Sit slightly forward in a way that allows you to be both comfortable and alert.

Make sure that you arrive early and well prepared for the interview.

Try to achieve eye contact with each member of the panel and as much as possible address your answer directly to the panel member who asked the question (glancing regularly at the others), not up in the air or to a piece of furniture. Most importantly, try to relax and enjoy the interview. This will help you to project an open, cheerful personality.

Finally, watch out for irritating mannerisms. These are easily checked if you videotape a mock interview. The interviewers will not listen to what you are saying if they are all watching to see when you are next going to scratch your left ear with your right thumb!

WHAT HAPPENS NEXT

When you have left the room the person chairing the interview panel will discuss your performance with the other members and will make a recommendation to the Dean. The recommendation will be one of the following:

- Accept
- Discuss further/waiting list
- Reject.

Accept means that you will receive a conditional or unconditional offer, usually the standard one. (See Chapter 6).

Discuss further means that you are borderline and may or may not receive an offer depending on the quality of the applicants seen by other interview panels. If, having been classified as 'Discuss further', you are unlucky and receive a rejection, the medical school may put you on an official or unofficial waiting list. The people on the waiting list are the first to be considered in Clearing. In 2003, UCAS introduced a scheme called Extra, which allows applicants who have been rejected by all of the institutions to which they applied a chance to approach other universities. Details can be found on the UCAS website.

Reject means that you have not been made an offer. You may be luckier at one of the other medical schools to which you have applied, or you may have to wait and try to obtain a place through Clearing.

The official notification of your fate will come to you from UCAS within a few weeks of the interview. If you have been rejected it is helpful to know whether you are on the waiting list and whether or not there is any point in applying again to that medical school. Understandably, the staff will be reluctant to talk to you about your performance, but most medical schools will discuss your application with your UCAS referee if he or she rings them to ask what advice should now be given to you. It is well worth asking your referee to make that telephone call.

3

Results day

The A level results will arrive at your school on the third Thursday in August. The medical schools will have received them a few days earlier. You must make sure that you are at home on the day the results are published. Don't wait for the school to post the results slip to you. Get the staff to tell you the news as soon as possible. If you need to act to secure a place, you may have to act quickly. This chapter will take you through the steps you should follow – for example you may need to use the Clearing system because you have good grades but no offer. It also explains what to do if your grades are disappointing.

WHAT TO DO IF THINGS GO WRONG DURING THE EXAMS

If something happens when you are preparing for or actually taking the exams which prevents you from doing your best, you must notify both the exam board and the medical schools that have made you offers. This notification will come best from your headteacher and should include your UCAS number. Send it off at once: it is no good waiting for disappointing results and then telling everyone that you felt ghastly at the time but said nothing to anyone. Exam boards can give you special consideration if the appropriate forms are sent to them by the school, along with supporting evidence.

Your extenuating circumstances must be convincing. A 'slight sniffle' won't do! If you really are sufficiently ill to be unable to prepare for the exams or to perform effectively during them, you must consult your GP and obtain a letter describing your condition.

The other main cause of under-performance is distressing events at home. If a member of your immediate family is very seriously ill, you should explain this to your head-teacher and ask him or her to write to the examiners and medical schools.

With luck, the exam board will give you the benefit of the doubt if your marks fall on a grade border. Equally, you can hope that the medical school will allow you to slip one grade below the conditional offer. If things work out badly, then the fact that you declared extenuating circumstances should ensure that you are treated sympathetically when you reapply through UCAS.

The medical school admissions departments are well organised and efficient, but they are staffed by human beings. If there were extenuating circumstances that could have affected your exam performance and that were brought to their notice in June, it is a good idea to ask them to review the relevant letters shortly before the exam results are published.

WHAT TO DO IF YOU HOLD AN OFFER AND GET THE GRADES

If you previously received a conditional offer and your grades equal or exceed that offer, congratulations! You can relax and wait for your chosen medical school to send you joining instructions. One word of warning: you cannot assume that grades of AAC satisfy an ABB offer. This is especially true if the C grade is in Chemistry. Read on.

WHAT TO DO IF YOU HAVE GOOD GRADES BUT NO OFFER

Every year, UCAS statistics reveal that around 300 people get into medical school through Clearing. However, that does not mean that all of these were students who were not holding offers but who nevertheless gained places – many of them were students who narrowly missed their offers, but were given places based on their strong performance at interview or because of extenuating circumstances. Table 1 in Chapter 6 shows that very few schools keep places open and, of those that do, most will choose to allow applicants who hold a conditional offer to slip a grade rather than dust off a reserve list of those they interviewed but didn't make an offer to. Still less are they likely to consider applicants who appear out of the blue – however high their grades. That said, it is likely that every summer a few medical schools will have enough unfilled places to consider a Clearing-style application.

If you hold three A grades but were rejected when you applied through UCAS, you need to let the medical schools know that you are out there. The best way to do this is by email. Contact details are listed in the *UCAS Directory*. If you live nearby, you can always deliver a letter in person, talk to the office staff and hope that your application will stand out from the rest.

Set out on the following page is sample text for a email/fax/letter. Don't copy it word for word!

Don't forget that your UCAS referee may be able to help you. Try to persuade him or her to ring the admissions officers on your behalf – he or she will find it easier to get through than you will. If your referee is unable/unwilling to ring, then he or she should, at least, email a note in support of your application. It is best if both emails arrive at the medical school at the same time.

If you are applying to a medical school that did not receive your UCAS application, ask your referee to email or fax a copy of the form. In general, it is best to persuade the medical school to invite you to arrange for the UCAS application to be sent.

If, despite your most strenuous efforts, you are unsuccessful, you need to consider applying again (see below). The other alternative is to use the Clearing system to obtain a place on a degree course related to medicine and hope to be accepted on the medical course after you graduate. This option is described on page 70.

---

1 Melchester Road
Melchester MC2 3EF
0123 456 7890
15 August 2008

Miss M D Whyte
Admissions Officer
Melchester Hospital Medical School
Hospital Road
Melchester MC1 4JK

Dear Miss Whyte

UCAS no 08-123456-7

I have just received my A level results, which were:
Biology A, Chemistry A, English A.
I also have a B grade in AS Philosophy.

You may remember that I applied to Melchester but was rejected after interview/was rejected without an interview. I am still very keen to study medicine at Melchester and hope that you will consider me for any places which may now be available.

My head teacher supports my application and is emailing you a reference. Should you wish to contact him, his details are: Mr C Harrow, tel: 0123 456 7891, fax: 0123 456 7892, email: c.harrow@melchester.sch.uk.

I can be contacted at the above address and could attend an interview at short notice.

Yours sincerely

L M Johnson

Lucy Johnson (Miss)

WHAT TO DO IF YOU HOLD AN OFFER BUT MISS THE GRADES

THE OPTIONS

If you have only narrowly missed the required grades (this includes the AAC grade case described above), it is important that you and your referee contact the medical school to put your case before you are rejected. Sample text for another email/fax/letter follows below.

---

1 Melchester Road
Melchester MC2 3EF
0123 456 7890
15 August 2008

Miss M D Whyte
Admissions Officer
Melchester Hospital Medical School
Hospital Road
Melchester MC1 4JK

Dear Miss Whyte

UCAS no 08-123456-7

I have just received my A level results, which were:
Chemistry A, Biology A, English C.
I also have a B grade in AS Philosophy.

I hold a conditional offer from Melchester of ABB and I realise that my grades may not meet that offer. Nevertheless I am still determined to study medicine and I hope you will be able to find a place for me this year.

May I remind you that at the time of the exams I was recovering from glandular fever. A medical certificate was sent to you in June by my head teacher.

My head teacher supports my application and is emailing you a reference. Should you wish to contact him, his details are: Mr C Harrow, tel: 0123 456 7891, fax: 0123 456 7892, email: c.harrow@melchester.sch.uk.

I can be contacted at the above address and could attend an interview at short notice.

Yours sincerely

L M Johnson

Lucy Johnson (Miss)

If this is unsuccessful, you need to consider retaking your A levels and applying again (see below). The other alternative is to use the Clearing system to obtain a place on a degree course related to medicine and hope to apply to the medical course after you graduate. This option is described on page 70.

RETAKING YOUR A LEVELS

The grade requirements for retake candidates are normally higher than for first timers (usually AAA). You should retake any subject where your first result was below B and you should aim for an A grade in any subject you do retake. It is often necessary to retake a B grade, especially in Chemistry – take advice from the college that is preparing you for the retake.

Most AS and some A2 units can be taken in January sittings, and some boards offer other sittings. This means that a January retake is often technically possible, although you should check carefully before taking up this option, since there may be complications because of the number of times units/modules have already been taken, and because of coursework.

The timescale for your retake will depend on:

■ The grades you obtained first time
■ The syllabuses you studied.

If you simply need to improve one subject by one or two grades and can retake the exam on the same syllabus in January, then the short retake course is the logical option.

If, on the other hand, your grades were DDE and you took your exams through a board which has no mid-year retakes for the units that you require, you probably need to spend another year on your retakes. You would find it almost impossible to master syllabus changes in three subjects and achieve an increase of nine or ten grades within the 17 weeks that are available for teaching between September and January.

Independent sixth-form colleges provide specialist advice and teaching for students considering A level retakes.

Interviews to discuss this are free and carry no obligation to enrol on a course, so it is worth taking the time to talk to their staff before you embark on A level retakes.

REAPPLYING TO MEDICAL SCHOOL

Many medical schools discourage retake candidates (see Tables 2 and 3 in Chapter 6) so the whole business of applying again needs careful thought, hard work and a bit of luck.

The choice of medical schools for your UCAS application is narrower than it was the first time round. Don't apply to the medical schools that discourage retakers unless there really are special, extenuating circumstances to explain your disappointing grades. Among the excuses that will not wash are:

> *I wasn't feeling too good on the day of the practical exam, knocked over my Bunsen and torched the answer book.*

> *My dog had been ill for a week before my exams and only recovered after the last paper (and I've got a vet's certificate to prove it).*

> *I'd spent the month before the exams condensing my notes on to small cards so that I could revise effectively. Two days before the exams our house was broken into and the burglar trod on my notes as he climbed through the window. The police took them away for forensic examination and didn't give them back until after the last paper (and I've got a note from the CID to prove it).*

Some reasons are acceptable to even the most fanatical opponents of retake candidates:

- Your own illness
- The death or serious illness of a very close relative.

Consider, in addition, your age when you took the exams. Most medical schools will accept that a candidate who was well under the age of 18 on the date of sitting A levels may deserve another attempt without being branded a 'retaker'.

These are just guidelines and the only safe method of finding out if a medical school will accept you is to ask them. Text for a typical email/fax/letter is set out below. Don't follow it slavishly and do take the time to write to several medical schools before you make your final choice.

---

1 Melchester Road
Melchester MC2 3EF
0123 456 7890
15 August 2007

Miss M D Whyte
Admissions Officer
Melchester Hospital Medical School
Hospital Road
Melchester MC1 4JK

Dear Miss Whyte

Last year's UCAS no 08-123456-7

I am writing to ask your advice because I am about to complete my UCAS application and would very much like to apply to Melchester.

You may remember that I applied to you last year and received an offer of AAB/was rejected after interview/was rejected without an interview.

I have just received my A level results, which were:
Biology C, Chemistry D, English E.
I also have a B grade in AS Psychology.

I was aged 17 years and six months at the time of taking these exams.

I plan to retake Chemistry in January after a 17-week course and English over a year. If necessary, I will retake Biology from January to June. I am confident that I can push these subjects up to A grades overall.

What worries me is that I have heard that some medical schools do not consider retake candidates even when the exams were taken under the age of 18 and relatively high grades achieved. I am very keen not to waste a slot on my UCAS application (or your time) by applying to schools that will reject me purely because I am retaking.

I am very keen to come to Melchester, and would be extremely grateful for any advice that you can give me.

Yours sincerely

L M Johnson

Lucy Johnson (Miss)

Notice that the format of your letter should be:

- Opening paragraph
- Your exam results – set out clearly and with no omissions
- Any extenuating circumstances – a brief statement
- Your retake plan – including the timescale
- A request for help and advice
- Closing formalities.

Make sure that your letter is brief, clear and well presented. If you send a letter rather than an email, you can word-process it, if you wish, but you should write *'Dear Sir/Madam'* and *'Yours faithfully'* by hand. If you have had any previous contact with the admissions staff you will be able to write *'Dear Miss Whyte'* and *'Yours sincerely'*. Even if you go to this trouble the pressure on medical schools in the autumn is such that you may receive no more than a photocopied standard reply to the effect that, if you apply, your application will be considered or an email directing you to the relevant part of their website.

Apart from the care needed in making the choice of medical school, the rest of the application procedure is as described in the first section of this book.

**For up-to-date information on
medicine and medical schools, go to
www.mpw.co.uk/getintomed**

Non-standard Applications

So far, this book has been concerned with the 'standard' applicant: the UK resident who is studying at least two science subjects at A level and who is applying from school or who is retaking immediately after disappointing A levels. However, medical schools accept a small number of applicants who do not have this 'standard' background. The main non-standard categories are outlined in this chapter.

THOSE WHO HAVE NOT STUDIED SCIENCE A LEVELS

If you decide that you would like to study medicine after having already started on a combination of A levels that does not fit the subject requirements for entry to medical school, you can apply for the 'pre-medical course'. This is offered at seven university faculties of medicine.

The course covers elements of chemistry, biology and physics and lasts one academic year. It leads to the first MB qualification for which science A levels provide exemption.

If your pre-med application is rejected, you will have to spend a further two years taking science A levels at a sixth-form college. Alternatively, independent sixth-form colleges offer one-year A level courses and certain subjects can be covered from scratch in a single year. However, only very able students can cover A level Chemistry and Biology in a single year with good results. You should discuss your particular circumstances with the staff of a number of colleges in order to select the course that will prepare you to achieve the A level subjects you need at the grades you require.

OVERSEAS STUDENTS

Most medical schools are limited by government quota to accepting only 7.5% of overseas students each year. In the academic year 2005/2006 the tuition fees charged to these students were typically between £12,000 and £16,000 per year for the pre-clinical courses and between £21,000 and £26,000 per year for the clinical courses.

The competition for the few places available to overseas students is fierce and you would be wise to discuss your application informally with the medical school before submitting your UCAS application. Many medical schools give preference to students who do not have adequate provision for training in their own countries. You should contact the medical schools individually for advice.

Information about qualifications can be obtained from British Council offices or British Embassies.

MATURE STUDENTS AND GRADUATES

In recent years the options available for mature students have increased enormously. There is a growing awareness that older students often represent a 'safer' option for medical schools because they are likely to be more committed to medicine and less likely to drop out, and are able to bring to the medical world many skills and experiences that 18-year-olds sometimes lack. In general, there are two types of mature applicant:

- Those who have always wanted to study medicine but who failed to get into medical school when they applied from school in the normal way
- Those who came to the idea later on in life, often having embarked on a totally different career.

The first type of mature applicant has usually followed a degree course in a subject related to medicine and has obtained a good grade (minimum 2.1). These students have an uphill path into medicine because their early failure tends to prejudice the selectors. Nevertheless, they do not have the problem of taking science A levels at a late stage in their education. A few years ago, applicants in this position almost always had to go back to the beginning (sometimes even having to resit A levels) and then apply to the medical schools for the standard five-/six-year courses.

The second category of mature student is often of more interest to the medical school selectors and interviewers. Applications are welcomed from people who have achieved success in other careers and who can bring a breadth of experience to the medical school and to the profession.

Options available for mature students are summarised below. The second part of the chapter then examines each option in more detail.

APPLICANTS WITH A LEVELS THAT SATISFY MEDICAL SCHOOLS' STANDARD OFFERS
- Five-/six-year courses in the normal way.

APPLICANTS WITH A LEVELS THAT DO NOT SATISFY STANDARD OFFERS
This could include arts A levels, or grades too low.

- Retake/pick up new A levels at sixth-form college.
- Six-year pre-medical/medical courses (First MB/ChB pre-medical entry), available at Bristol, Dundee, Edinburgh, King's, Manchester, Sheffield and Cardiff. These courses are usually given the code A104 by UCAS. They include a foundation (pre-medical) year and are designed for students without science A level backgrounds. They should not be confused with the six-year (usually A100) courses offered by many medical schools, which include an intercalated BSc. The A100 courses require science A levels.
- Access courses.

GRADUATES

- Four-year graduate entry courses
- Five-/six-year courses in the normal way
- Six-year pre-medical/medical courses
- Access courses.

MATURE STUDENTS WITH NO FORMAL A LEVEL OR EQUIVALENT QUALIFICATIONS

- A levels, then five-/six-year courses in the normal way
- Access courses.

Mature students and graduates are faced with many decisions on the route towards becoming a doctor. Not only do they have to decide which course or combination of courses might be suitable, but in many cases they also have to try to gauge how best to juggle the conflicting demands of study, financial practicalities and their families. As an illustration of this, take the case of Sam Kirkwood.

When Sam was considering what A levels to take, she decided to follow the arts/humanities route. She decided not to consider medicine as a career although she came from a medical background. She chose A levels in English, History and French and, following a gap year, she took up her place at Cambridge to read English Literature. During her time at Cambridge she gained work experience in the City, and after she graduated she joined the investment bank UBS as a graduate trainee. She spent five years there and then moved to another investment bank. During this time she had a baby.

Her interest in medicine was triggered – as is often the case – by television programmes such as *ER*. The fly-on-the-wall documentary, *Help! I'm a Doctor*, which followed four graduates as they embarked upon their medical training, was also an influence. At that stage she started to do some research. She spoke to friends who had gone into medicine as mature students, she contacted medical schools and went to open days. The admissions department at St George's was particularly helpful and put her in contact with students who had done something similar.

The websites www.admissionsforum.co.uk and
www.medschoolguide.co.uk also provided information.

Sam had to decide whether to apply to graduate courses
that did not require a science background, to follow an
Access course or to start the process by taking science A
levels in a year. She decided against Access courses since
the ones that allowed applications to a range of medical
schools (such as the course at the College of West Anglia)
– rather than those aimed at a particular medical school –
would have required her to move from London, which
was not possible because of family considerations. To give
herself the broadest set of options, Sam decided to go to
an independent sixth-form college to take A level
Chemistry and Biology in a year, and to apply to a
combination of four-year and five-/six-year courses.

Sam's medical school interview questions were typical
of those faced by mature students and graduates. The
interviewers were interested in:

- Why she had decided to change direction
- What she had done to convince herself that this was
  the right option for her
- What her career had given her in the way of personal
  qualities that were relevant to medicine
- What financial arrangements she had made to fund
  her studies
- Whether she had found it difficult studying A levels
  alongside 18-year-olds.

Sam opted for the A level route for three reasons: to give
herself a solid science background; to get used to studying
with younger students; and to give herself a year to make
sure that this was the right option for her. She gained a
place at UCL, and started her course in 2005.

PERSONAL STATEMENT

For mature applicants, the UCAS personal statement
needs to be carefully structured. In most cases, insuffi-
cient space is allowed for the amount of information
necessary to present a convincing case. It is usually
advisable for mature applicants to send a detailed CV and

covering letter direct to the medical schools once their UCAS number has been received.

For mature applicants, the personal statement should be structured as follows:

1 | Brief career and educational history – in note form or bullet points if necessary
2 | Reasons for the change of direction
3 | What the candidate has done to investigate medicine
4 | Brief details of achievements, interests, etc – again, note form or bullet points are fine.

TIP: The most important thing to bear in mind is that you must convince the selectors that you are serious about the change in direction, and that your decision to apply to study medicine is not a spur-of-the-moment reaction to dissatisfaction with your current job or studies. A useful exercise is to try to imagine that you are the person who will read the personal statement in order to decide whether to interview or to reject without interview. Does your personal statement contain sufficient indication of thorough research, preparation and long-term commitment? If it does not, you will be rejected. As a rough guide, at least half of it should cover your reasons for applying for a medical course and the preparation and research that you have undertaken. The further back in time you can demonstrate that you started to plan your application, the stronger it will be.

ACCESS COURSES

A number of colleges of further education offer Access to Medicine courses. The best-known and most successful of these is the course at the College of West Anglia, in King's Lynn. Primarily (but not exclusively) aimed at health professionals, the course covers Biology, Chemistry, Physics and other medically related topics and lasts one year. Most medical schools will accept students who have successfully completed the course. Contact details can be found at the end of the book.

FOUR-YEAR GRADUATE COURSES

Often known as GEPs (Graduate Entry Programmes), these are given the code A101 or A102 by UCAS. The biggest change in medical school entry in recent years has been the development of these graduate entry schemes. The first medical schools to introduce accelerated courses specifically for graduates were St George's Hospital Medical School and Leicester/Warwick (which has since separated into two separate medical schools). Courses can be divided into two types: those for graduates with a medically-related degree; and those that accept graduates with degrees in any discipline.

The following medical schools run Graduate Entry Programmes (UCAS code A101/A102), further details of which can be found on the UCAS website:

- Birmingham
- Bristol
- Cambridge
- King's
- Leicester
- Liverpool
- Newcastle
- Nottingham
- Oxford
- Queen Mary
- Southampton
- St George's
- Swansea
- Warwick.

The King's course differs from the others listed above, as it is also available to healthcare professionals with equivalent academic qualifications. The first year of the course is taught in London or in Kent. Students then join the other King's MB BS students for the remaining three years.

GAMSAT

Four medical schools use the GAMSAT (Graduate Australian Medical School Admissions Test). For GAMSAT enquiries, email gamsat@ucas.ac.uk or see www.gamsat.co.uk. Candidates sit the GAMSAT examination in September, and those with the best all-round scores are then called for interview. The GAMSAT examination consists of three papers:

1 | Reasoning in humanities and social sciences (75 multiple-choice questions)

2 | Written communication (two essays)
3 | Reasoning in biological and physical sciences
(110 multiple-choice questions: 40% biology, 40%
chemistry, 20% physics).

The medical schools which use the GAMSAT examination
for their graduate courses are:

- St George's Hospital Medical School
  (www.sgul.ac.uk/students/gep)
- Nottingham Medical School
  (www.nottingham.ac.uk/mhs/GEM)
- University of Wales, Swansea
  (www.gemedicine.swan.ac.uk).

Peninsula Medical School (www.pms.ac.uk) also uses the
GAMSAT for anyone who has not sat A levels in the last
two years. Peninsula does not offer the A101 course.

MSAT

Three medical schools – King's, Queen Mary and
Warwick – require students who are applying for A101 or
A102 courses to sit the Medical Schools Admissions Test
(MSAT). This test, which also takes place in November,
consists of three sections:

1 | Critical reasoning (65 minutes – 45 questions)
2 | Interpersonal understanding (55 minutes – 55 questions)
3 | Written communication (60 minutes – two essays).

Further details can be found on www.ucas.com/tests/
msat.html and www.acer.edu.au/tests/university/msat.

**STUDYING
OUTSIDE
THE UK**

If you are unsuccessful in gaining a place at one of the UK
medical schools, and do not want to follow the graduate-
entry path, you might want to look at other options.
There are medical schools throughout the world that will
accept A level students, but the important issue is
whether or not you would be able, should you wish to do
so, to practise in the UK upon qualification. Popular
courses for UK students are:

- ■ **St Matthew's**, in the Cayman Islands. This is a five-year course (one year 'pre-med' course at the University of Sussex, two years at St Matthew's, and two years in either the US or the UK).
- ■ **Royal College of Surgeons** in Dublin. Students from countries within the European Union who qualify gain limited registration from the GMC.
- ■ **St George's University School of Medicine** in Grenada (West Indies). Students who wish to practise in the UK can spend part of the clinical stage of the course in a range of hospitals in the UK including King's in London. To practise in the UK, students sit the PLAB (Professional and Linguistic Assessments Board) test to gain limited registration; for more information see www.gmc-uk.org/doctors/plab/index.asp. Clinical experience can also be gained in hospitals in the US, allowing students to practise there as well. A high proportion of the medical school teachers have worked in UK universities and medical schools.
- ■ Medical courses taught in English, at **Charles University** in Prague and at other universities in the Czech Republic.

In addition to the medical schools attached to UK universities, there are a number of institutions offering medical degree courses that are taught in the UK but are accredited by overseas universities – mostly based in the Caribbean, Russia or Africa. If you are considering these, you must ensure that you are fully satisfied that the courses are bona fide and that the qualification you received would allow you to practise in the UK (or anywhere else in the world!). Details of these medical schools can be found in Chapter 6.

5

CURRENT ISSUES

NATIONAL HEALTH SERVICE

The National Health Service was set up in 1948 to provide healthcare free of charge at the point of delivery. That is not to say that, if you fell ill in 1947, you necessarily had to pay for your treatment. Accident and emergency services had been developed and had coped well with the demands of a population under bombardment during the Second World War. Some hospitals were ancient, wealthy charitable institutions owning valuable assets such as property in London. These hospitals charged patients who could afford to pay and treated others without charge. Doctors often worked on the same basis. Other hospitals were owned and funded by local authorities. The system was supported by low-cost insurance schemes, which were often fully or partially funded by employers.

The problem perceived by the architects of the NHS was that poorer members of society were reluctant to seek diagnosis and treatment. By funding the system out of a national insurance scheme to which every employer and employee would contribute, the government conferred on all citizens (whether employed or not) the right to free healthcare without the stigma of charity.

The service has undergone a number of reforms since 1948, but by far the most fundamental was introduced by the Conservative government in 1990. In recent years, the Labour government has made further changes to the system. It is important to understand what these reforms were, why they were thought to be necessary and what the outcome has been.

By the late 1980s it was clear to the government that the NHS could not function in the future without a substantial increase in funding. The fundamental reason for this was an expected reduction in the taxpayer's contribution, linked to an anticipated increase in demand for healthcare. Let's see why this was so.

INCREASED DEMAND
By 1990:

- The NHS had become a victim of its own success: when the service saved the life of a patient who would normally have died, that person survived to have another illness, to receive more treatment and incur more expense for the NHS.
- The number of life-prolonging procedures/ treatments/drugs had increased as a result of developments in medical science.
- The cost of these sophisticated procedures/ treatments/drugs was high, and increasing at a rate faster than inflation.
- The cost of staff had increased because, while pay rates had risen, the hours worked for that pay had fallen. At the same time, the cost of training staff in the new procedures and equipment was high.
- Patient expectations had grown. Knowledge of the new procedures/treatment/drugs meant that patients demanded access to them without delay.

THE 1990 REFORMS
The government believed that there were inefficiencies in the NHS, the removal of which would ease the pressure on funding, and they resolved to use market forces (in other words, to introduce an element of price competition) to overcome these inefficiencies.

For a market to work, you need providers (of goods and services) and purchasers. The purchasers need the freedom to choose between several providers, and to have extensive information about the price and quality of the goods or services offered by each provider.

Logically, therefore, the government should have given us back our taxes and left us free to shop around for the best deals. We could have chosen the hospital that offered us the cheapest hip replacement operation and kept the change. Of course that isn't what they did; governments give back taxes as willingly as water flows uphill and, anyway, there is a significant section of the population that pays no tax. Instead, they asked the District Health Authorities (DHAs) and the general practitioners (GPs) to act as purchasers on our behalf and, by doing so, they began to water down the principle of the market and, arguably, its benefits.

The scheme was designed to work as follows:

HOSPITAL TRUSTS

Before the reforms, hospitals were operated and funded by DHAs. The government wanted the DHAs, and later the GPs, to become 'purchasers' and the hospitals to become 'providers' in the new health marketplace. Hospitals (or groups of hospitals) were told to form themselves into NHS Trusts, which would act as independent businesses but with a number of crucial (and market-diluting) differences. They were to calculate the cost of all the treatment they offered and to price it at cost to the GP purchasers. In addition, and on the assumption that there were inefficiencies within the system that needed rooting out, they were told to reduce this cost by 3% annually.

GP FUNDHOLDERS

GPs were encouraged to become 'fundholders'. Historically, GPs have received money according to a formula based largely on the number and age of the patients registered with them. In addition, they were now to receive annually a sum of money (the fund) based on the cost of hospital treatment and prescribed drugs received by their patients. They were to be empowered to buy hospital treatment for their patients at the best price they could find. If they could do this at a total cost lower than the fund, they could invest the surplus in their 'practice' for the benefit of their patients. (The fundholding scheme was not designed to cover the cost of acute emergency work.)

HOSPITALS

The effect of the reforms was dramatic and largely unpopular. Particularly unpopular was the assertion that old hospitals in areas of low population density were not economically viable and should be closed. St Bartholomew's Hospital in the City of London was an example. Suddenly there were winners and losers in a world that had considered itself removed from the pressures of commercial life.

CARE IN THE COMMUNITY

Another controversial aspect of the NHS reforms, and one that has had a great impact on GP workload, has been the decision to transfer as many patients as possible from secondary (hospital) care to primary (community) care. In practice, this has led to the decision to close down many of the old mental hospitals and other long-stay units and release the patients to be 'cared for in the community'. The argument is that it is inhuman to lock up patients in 'Victorian' institutions when they could enjoy quasi-normal lives.

The system has worked well in some cases, but the release of schizophrenics who, free of close supervision, have failed to take the drugs that control their dangerous condition is a cause of concern. It has been estimated that, on average, two people are murdered every month by mentally ill people who have been released into the community. It is argued that community care can only function properly if it is properly funded, and that proper funding would be more expensive than building new secure hospitals for the mentally ill. The Mental Health Foundation estimates that an extra £540m is needed annually to provide adequate care for the 300,000 severely mentally ill.

THE 1997 REFORMS

The Government White Paper of 1997 (entitled *The New NHS: Modern, Dependable*) made a number of suggestions:

- The replacement of the internal market with **'integrated care'**. This involved the formation of 500 Primary Care Groups typically covering 100,000 patients – bringing together family doctors and community nurses – replacing GP fundholding, which ceased to exist in 1999.
- **NHSnet**. Every GP surgery and hospital would be connected via the internet. It would mean less waiting for prescriptions, quicker appointments, and less delay in getting results of tests.
- **New services** for patients. Everyone with suspected cancer would be guaranteed an appointment with a specialist within two weeks.
- **NHS Direct**. A 24-hour nurse-led telephone advice and information service.
- **Savings**. £1 billion savings from cutting paperwork would be ploughed back into patient care.

RATIONING AND NICE

Any suggestion of 'rationing' of healthcare causes the public great concern. The issue hit the headlines in January 1999 when Frank Dobson (the then Health Secretary) announced that, because of lack of funds, the use of Viagra (an anti-impotence drug) would be rationed: the NHS would only provide Viagra for cases of impotence arising from a small number of named causes. For example, a man whose impotence was caused by diabetes could be prescribed Viagra on the NHS, whereas if the cause was kidney failure, he would have to pay for the drug privately.

The publicity surrounding Viagra alerted people to other issues, in particular rationing by age and postcode prescribing.

RATIONING BY AGE

The charity Age Concern commissioned a Gallup poll which, they claimed, revealed that older people were being denied healthcare and being poorly treated in both primary and secondary care. The BMA responded by arguing that people of different ages require different patterns of treatment or referral. They cited the example of the progression of cancer, which is more rapid in younger people and often needs more aggressive radiotherapy, chemotherapy or surgery.

POSTCODE PRESCRIBING

Until the formation of NICE (see below) in 1999, health authorities received little guidance in what drugs and treatments to prescribe. Some well-publicised cases revealed large differences in the range of drugs and treatments available between regions (hence the term 'postcode rationing'). Beta interferon, a drug that extends the remission from multiple sclerosis (MS) in some patients, was prescribed by some health authorities but not by others, and the press highlighted cases where patients were forced to pay thousands of pounds a year to buy the drug privately, when others at an identical stage of MS, but who lived a few miles away, received the drug on the NHS.

Another well-publicised issue is that of infertility treatment (IVF). Whether or not treatment on the NHS is provided depends very much on which part of the country you live in. Across the country, about 1 in 5 infertile couples receive IVF treatment (although this figure is much higher in some areas). In February 2004 the government announced that the target is to rise to 4 in 5, and that the provision will be uniform across the country. Although this may sound very encouraging to prospective parents, there is (of course!) a downside: at the moment, infertile couples who are eligible for IVF receive up to three sets of treatment, giving a 1 in 2 chance of conception. Under the new arrangements, couples will have only one set of treatment, reducing the chance of conception to 1 in 4. After that, they have to pay for the treatment themselves.

NICE

The National Institute for Clinical Excellence (NICE) was set up as a Special Health Authority in April 1999.

In April 2005 it merged with the Health Development Agency to become the new National Institute for Health and Clinical Excellence, which is still known as NICE. Its role is to provide the NHS with guidance on individual health technologies (for instance, drugs) and treatments. In the words of the Chairman of NICE, Professor Sir Michael Rawlins, 'NICE is about taking a look at what's available, identifying what works and helping the NHS to get more of what works into practice'. The government has acknowledged that there are variations in the quality of care available to different patients in different parts of the country, and it hopes that the guidance that NICE can provide will reduce these differences. In a speech explaining the role of NICE, the Chairman said that it has been estimated that, on average, health professionals should be reading 19 medical and scientific articles each day if they are to keep up to date – in future, they can read the NICE bulletins instead.

It is unlikely, however, that NICE will end the controversies surrounding new treatments, since it will be making recommendations based not only on clinical effectiveness, but also on cost-effectiveness – something that is very difficult to judge. A good example of a situation where a drug can be clinically effective but not cost-effective is the case of the first drug that NICE reviewed, a new treatment for influenza called zanamivir (Relenza). Despite a hefty publicity campaign when it was introduced, NICE advised doctors and health authorities not to prescribe the drug. NICE argued that although the clinical trials showed that, if taken within 48 hours of the onset of symptoms, the duration of flu is reduced by 24 hours, there was no evidence that it would prevent the 3,000–4,000 deaths a year which result from complications from flu.

In addition to Relenza, NICE has investigated the effectiveness of many treatments including:

- Hip replacement joints
- Therapy for depression

- Treatments for Crohn's disease
- IVF treatment (see above)
- Drugs for hepatitis C
- Surgery for corectal cancer
- Drugs for breast cancer (taxanes)
- Drugs for brain cancer (temozolomides)
- Identification and management of eating disorders such as anorexia nervosa
- Laser treatment in eye surgery
- Treatments for obesity.

Full details of the results of these and other investigations can be found on the NICE website (www.nice.org.uk).

2004 REFORMS – FOUNDATION HOSPITALS

'What will they ask me about the NHS?' is a common question from students about to attend medical school interviews. To judge by recent feedback, the most popular topic is foundation hospitals, the government's latest reform of the NHS. NHS Foundation Trusts, to give them their proper title, are being established to provide greater ownership and involvement of patients in their local hospitals. A board of governors is elected locally and has a large say in the running of the hospitals. Direct elections for the board of governors should (it is hoped) ensure that services are directed more closely at the local community. Hospitals have been allowed to apply for Trust status since April 2004. There are now 52 Foundation Trusts.

If you listen to the news or read the newspapers you will be aware that not everyone is happy with the idea of Foundation Trusts. Critics argue that a 'two-tier' NHS will result, with the rich and powerful Foundation Trusts able to offer higher pay to staff, at the expense of other (less wealthy) hospitals. There are also concerns that Foundation Trusts will treat too many private patients in order to increase income. This, say critics, will be an inevitable outcome of a system where Foundation Trusts can borrow money from the government to improve services and facilities. First drafts of the government's bill referred to Foundation Trusts as 'companies', raising fears of the privatisation of the NHS.

2006 REFORMS – PATIENT CHOICE

You might also be asked about the recent NHS reforms relating to patient choice and payment by results, both of which came into force in the first half of 2006. Patients are now able to choose the hospital that will treat them for non-emergency cases from a list of four or more. The government is also introducing a new funding system in which hospitals are paid per patient treated, and more private hospitals will be paid by the NHS for operations on NHS patients. More information on these reforms is available at www.dh.gov.uk/PolicyAndGuidance/fs/en, and a good overview of the issues surrounding patient choice can be found at http://news.bbc.co.uk/1/hi/health/4746573.stm.

NHS SPENDING

- Since 1996, the NHS budget has risen from about £35 billion to over £80 billion.
- The percentage of GDP spent on healthcare in the UK has risen from below 7% in 1996 to nearly 9%, bringing the UK close to the top of the European health spending league. The European average is 8%.
- In the last five years, the NHS's spending on drugs has increased by almost 50% to £8 billion.
- Much of the increase in NHS funding has been spent on the workforce. GP and consultant pay is now among the highest in Europe, and it is estimated that about 40% of the £4.5 billion extra allocated to the NHS for 2006–7 will be spent on pay rises for NHS staff.
- The NHS employs 300,000 more staff now than it did in 1996. This has had the effect of reducing waiting lists and waiting times significantly (at least on paper).

BIRD FLU

The medical headlines in 2005 and early 2006 were dominated by fears about Avian Influenza A (H5N1) – also known as bird flu. Bird flu was first identified over 100 years ago, and is now known to affect all birds. Infected birds usually die. There are 15 known subtypes of bird flu, but the H5N1 strain is causing most concern. Type A influenza viruses have two important properties:

1 | During the replication process, any errors that occur are not repaired, so the genetic composition of the virus can change rapidly

2 | They can swap genetic material and merge with other type A influenza viruses – this is known as *antigenic shift*.

By January 2007, there had been 265 known cases of human infection, resulting in 159 deaths.

CONFIRMED CASES OF HUMAN H5N1 INFECTIONS

Country	Cases	Deaths
Azerbaijan	8	5
Cambodia	6	6
China	21	14
Djibouti	1	0
Egypt	18	10
Indonesia	76	57
Iraq	3	2
Thailand	25	17
Turkey	12	4
Vietnam	93	42
Total	263	157

Source: World Health Organization

It was thought that the virus could only be caught by direct contact with infected birds, but there is now evidence that human-to-human infection has occurred in Thailand and in Vietnam. Many governments have been stockpiling the antiviral drug Tamiflu, which limits symptoms and reduces the likelihood of the disease spreading. Worryingly, in December 2005 two people in Vietnam died of bird flu despite taking Tamiflu, raising fears that a Tamiflu-resistant strain has already evolved.

With such a small number of human deaths, these measures might be seen as an extraordinary overreaction. However, there are serious concerns that the H5N1 virus will combine with a strain of human flu, significantly increasing chances of human-to-human infection. Experts have predicted that, if this happens, there could be anything up to 50 million deaths worldwide. In 1918, an influenza pandemic caused an estimated 40 million deaths.

More information on avian influenza (including frequently asked questions) is available on the World Health Organization website – see www.who.int/csr/disease/avian_influenza.

MRSA

Ten years ago, most people had not heard of Methicillin-resistant Staphylococcus Aureus (MRSA). Now, horror stories abound (not all of them true) of people going into hospital to have an in-growing toenail treated, and having to stay for six months due to picking up an MRSA infection while there. It is estimated that 100,000 people each year catch the infection in UK hospitals, and that 5,000 of them die from it. The true extent of the problem is not really known. Government statistics show an official figure (that is, with MRSA recorded on the death certificate) of about 500 deaths from MRSA each year. This is not to say that there is any form of cover-up, it is simply that many people who are infected with MRSA in hospitals die from causes associated with the conditions that caused them to be in hospital in the first place.

The rate of infection in the UK is one of the highest in the world because of poor hygiene in hospitals. The infection spreads via staff who handle different patients throughout the day without washing their hands in between contact with one patient and the next, or because hospital wards are not cleaned properly. If the organisms that cause MRSA get into the blood system of people weakened by illness or age, through a wound or an injection, the effects can be very serious. Since the organism is resistant to many antibiotics, it is extremely difficult to treat.

In December 2004, the *Independent* reported that the NHS spends more than £1 billion a year in trying to prevent and treat the disease, and that over the last seven years the number of deaths from MRSA has doubled. The government has set a target of cutting the number of MRSA infections by 50 percent by 2008. Current indications are that this target will not be met.

GENES: MEDICAL AND ETHICAL ASPECTS

GENE THERAPY AND THE HUMAN GENOME PROJECT

Many illnesses are thought to be caused by defective genes: examples are cancer, cystic fibrosis and Alzheimer's disease. The defects may be hereditary or triggered by external factors such as ionising or solar radiation. The much-hyped dream of medical researchers, especially in the USA, is that the affected chromosomes could be repaired, allowing the body to heal itself.

To make this dream come true, scientists need to discover which gene is causing the problem and how to replace it with a healthy one. Great progress has been made in solving the first part of the puzzle thanks to a gigantic international research project known as the 'Human Genome Project', which has as its aim the identification of every human gene and an understanding of what effect it has. The full sequence was published in early 2,000. Many links have been made between diseases and specific genes but the techniques for replacing the defective genes have yet to prove themselves.

Two methods have been proposed:

- The healthy gene is incorporated in a retro-virus which, by its nature, splices its genetic material into the chromosomes of the host cell. The virus must first be treated in order to prevent it causing problems of its own. This 'denaturing' reduces the positive effects and, to date, the trials have been unconvincing.
- The healthy gene is incorporated in a fatty droplet which is sprayed into the nose in order to reach cells in the lining of the nose, air passages and lungs, or injected into the blood. It was hoped that this method would be effective against the single defective gene that causes cystic fibrosis but, again, the trials have yet to prove successful.

To make matters more complicated, it turns out that many of the illnesses which are genetic in origin are caused by defects in a wide number of genes, so the hoped-for magic bullet needs to be replaced by a magic cluster bomb – and that sounds suspiciously like the approach used by conventional pharmaceuticals. Since

1990, when gene therapy for humans began, about 300 clinical trials (involving diseases ranging from cystic fibrosis and heart disease to brain tumours) have been carried out, with very limited success.

GENETIC ENGINEERING

Genetic engineering is the name given to the manipulation of genes. There is a subtle difference between genetic engineering and gene therapy – specifically, that genetic engineering implies modification of the genes involved in reproduction. These modifications will then be carried over into future generations.

One of the reasons for considering these ideas is to try to produce enhanced performance in animals and plants. The possibility of applying genetic engineering to humans poses major ethical problems and, at present, experiments involving reproductive cells are prohibited. Nevertheless, one form of genetic engineering known as genetic screening is allowed. In this technique, an egg is fertilised in a test tube. When the embryo is two days old, one cell is removed and the chromosomes are tested to establish the sex and presence of gene defects. In the light of the tests, the parents decide whether or not to implant the embryo into the mother's womb.

Taken to its logical conclusion, this is the recipe for creating a breed of supermen. The superman concept may be morally acceptable when applied to race horses, but should it be applied to merchant bankers? How would we feel if a small, undemocratic state decided to apply this strategy to its entire population in order to obtain an economic advantage? Could we afford to ignore this challenge?

The fundamental argument against any policy that reduces variation in the human gene pool is that it is intrinsically dangerous because, in principle, it restricts the species' ability to adapt to new environmental challenges. Inability to adapt to an extreme challenge could lead to extinction of our species.

HUMAN CLONING

The breakthrough in cloning technology came in 1997 in the form of Dolly the sheep – see opposite. In February 2004, a group of South Korean scientists led by Dr Hwang announced that it had succeeded in cloning 30 human embryos to obtain stem cells, which could one day be used to treat diseases. Stem cells can develop into any type of cell in the human body and could be used to repair or replace damaged organs. They followed up this announcement in May 2005 by claiming that they had extracted cells from the cloned embryos that matched exactly the cells of 11 patients.

However, in December 2005, Seoul National University (where Dr Hwang and his team worked) concluded that the results were fabricated. Dr Hwang subsequently resigned, while maintaining that the scientific basis for his claims was still valid and that Korea led the world in stem-cell research.

There have been many claims in the past for the successful cloning of a human embryo. A number of doctors announced that they were either working on, or had successfully performed, human cloning. Names that may have come to your attention include an American, Dr Richard Seed; Dr Severino Antinori; Dr Panos Zavos (whose claim to have created the world's first cloned human embryo has yet to be substantiated); and an organisation called Clonaid founded by a religious cult.

It is important to make the distinction between reproductive cloning – the reproduction of genetically identical individuals – and therapeutic cloning, which does not involve the creation of genetically identical people, but uses the same techniques to produce replacement organs or to repair damaged organs.

The BMA 'considers unacceptable the notion of cloning whole humans and would not wish to see public policy develop in this way', but would like to see 'rational debate about the subject in order to ensure that public policies in this sphere can be supported by the strength of argument, and not solely by the strength of opinion'.

Therapeutic cloning could be used to produce embryonic stem cells which could then develop into specific types of tissue to repair or replace damaged organs. It is thought that stem cells could be used, for example, in the treatment of Parkinson's disease, to provide bone marrow for leukaemia treatment, to repair damaged heart muscles and to produce new skin for burns victims.

The BMA supports research into therapeutic cloning, 'including research using human embryos where necessary for the development of tissue for transplantation; and the development of methods of therapy for mitochondrial diseases'. In August 2004, scientists at the Newcastle NHS Fertility Cent92re were given a licence to create Europe's first cloned human embryos for research.

The BBC website (www.bbc.co.uk) provides a very good analysis of cloning issues.

Reasons why people may want human cloning:

- Infertility
- 'Recover' a child who has died
- Eugenics – to improve the human race
- Spare parts
- Research purposes.

Reasons why people are against human cloning:

- Health risks from mutation of genes
- Risks of abuse of the technology
- Ethical/religious reasons
- Emotional risks for cloned child.

DOLLY THE SHEEP AND THE ROSLIN INSTITUTE
Dolly, born at the Roslin Institute in Edinburgh, hit the headlines in February 1997 because she was the first mammal to be cloned from an adult cell. The importance of the birth is not the fact that a sheep had been cloned, as this had been done before using embryo cells, but that nobody had successfully taken adult cells – in this case from the udder of a six-year-old ewe – and cloned them.

Embryo cells have the potential to become complete embryos, but adult cells are differentiated – for instance, cells in the liver do the job of the liver – and so cloning is much more difficult. The process begins by starving cells of nutrients for a few days until they stop growing and dividing. The nucleus of one of these quiescent cells is then injected into a cell which had previously had its nucleus removed. A small electric current is used to kick the cell back into activity, and it is then put into the womb of a female sheep to grow. The egg now contains a full set of genes, as if it had been fertilised by a spermatozoa. It took 277 attempts to produce the first successful clone.

The difference between cloning and IVF treatment is that, in the latter, eggs are fertilised in a test tube (hence the so-called 'test-tube babies') using sperm from a male, and then placed in the uterus; whereas cloning involves the removal of the egg nucleus which is then replaced by the nucleus of the cell which is to be cloned. A cloned animal has only one parent.

Cloning could be an important source of genetically identical copies of organs, skin and blood cells for surgical use. The biotechnology company PPL Therapeutics, which worked with the Roslin scientists, hopes to use the cloning technique to produce sheep capable of generating the blood-clotting protein Factor IX in their milk. PPL estimates that 50 sheep would be enough to produce the £100m annual world demand for Factor IX. In January 2002 it was discovered that Dolly had arthritis. It is unusual for sheep under six years old to get arthritis in the rear legs, and this has raised fears that premature ageing could be a result of cloning. There is also chromosome evidence that Dolly aged faster than non-cloned sheep. If organs from cloned animals are one day going to be used for human transplants, will they age prematurely in the human's body?

On Friday 14 February 2003, Dolly was put down at the relatively young age of six years old, because the scientists decided that she would not recover from a progressive lung disease. Dr Harry Griffin, the acting Director at

Roslin, said, 'Sheep can live to 11 or 12 years of age, and lung diseases are common in older sheep, particularly those housed indoors. There is no evidence that cloning was a factor in Dolly contracting the disease.' The post-mortem did not uncover any other abnormalities.

In January 2007, the Roslin Institute announced that it had bred genetically modified chickens that lay eggs that contain medicinal proteins, from which drugs can be produced. The human genes within the chickens' DNA is passed from generation to generation. One of the breeds of chickens produces interferon, used to treat multiple sclerosis, and there are hopes that similar breeds could produce drugs that could treat arthritis and various forms of cancer.

WORLD HEALTH: RICH V POOR

In the industrialised world, infectious diseases are well under control. The main threats to health are circulatory diseases (such as heart disease and stroke), cancer, respiratory ailments and musculoskeletal conditions (rheumatic diseases and osteoporosis). All of these are diseases which tend to affect older people and, as life expectancy is increasing, they will become more prevalent in the future. Many are nutrition-related, where an unhealthy diet rich in saturated fats and processed foods leads to poor health.

In poorer countries, infectious diseases such as malaria, cholera, tuberculosis, hepatitis and HIV/AIDS are much more common. Malaria affects up to 500 million people a year and kills over a million; and 1.5 million die from tuberculosis. The UN estimated that in 2005, 4.9 million people were newly infected with HIV/AIDS and over 3 million people died from AIDS-related causes.

Infectious diseases go hand in hand with poverty: over-crowding, lack of clean water and poor sanitation all encourage the spread of diseases, and lack of money reduces the access to drugs and treatment. The WHO estimates that nearly 2 million deaths worldwide each year are attributable to unsafe water, sanitation and hygiene.

In its report on infectious diseases published in 2,000, the World Health Organization highlighted the problem of antimicrobial resistance. Although antimicrobial resistance is a natural phenomenon, the result of genetic mutation and 'survival of the fittest', the effect has been amplified in recent years by the misuse of antimicrobials. Many treatments which were effective ten years ago are no longer so, and it is a sobering thought that there have been no major new developments in antimicrobial drugs for 30 years. Given that new drugs take at least ten years to develop and test, it is easy to see that a problem is looming. The WHO's former director-general, Dr Gro Harlem Brundtland, was quoted in the health pages of the CNN website (www.cnn.com/health) as saying, 'We currently have effective medicines to cure almost every infectious disease, but we risk losing these valuable drugs and our opportunity to control infectious diseases.' Although it is commonly stated that the overuse of antimicrobials is the cause of the problem, it might be argued that it is actually the underuse that has done the damage since it is the pathogens that survive that cause the resistance.

Tourism also plays a part in the spread of diseases. The number of cases of malaria, yellow fever and other infectious diseases in developed countries is increasing as tourists catch the infections prior to returning to their own countries.

LIFE EXPECTANCY

The WHO uses an indicator called HALE (healthy average life expectancy) to compare the average life expectancies in each country in the world. HALE is based on life expectancy, but includes an adjustment for time spent in poor health. The HALE figures for developed countries are, of course, much higher than those for developing countries. Some 2002 examples can be seen below:

Country	HALE	Country	HALE
Japan	75.0	France	72.0
Switzerland	73.2	UK	70.6
Italy	72.7	USA	69.3

Country	HALE	Country	HALE
Afghanistan	35.5	Zimbabwe	33.6
Malawi	34.9	Lesotho	31.4

Source: World Health Organization

These figures could be the source of many interview questions:

- Why does Japan have the highest HALE?
- Why do Italy and France have higher HALEs than the UK?
- Why is the HALE in Afghanistan low?
- Why are most of the countries with the lowest HALE figures located in the middle and southern parts of Africa?

You can probably guess the answers to these, but if not, a discussion of these questions can be found on www.mpw.co.uk/getintomed, and further data is available at www3.who.int/whosis/core/core_select.cfm. The table below also provides some ideas.

HEALTHCARE EXPENDITURE

The table shows the 2003 figures for per capita government expenditure on health in US dollars and total health expenditure as a percentage of GDP.

Country	Per capita	Total
Japan	$2158	7.9%
United Kingdom	$2081	8.0%
India	$7	4.8%
Malawi	$5	9.3%

Source: World Health Organization

MMR

The MMR (measles, mumps and rubella) vaccine is a three-part vaccine given by injection to children when they reach the age of one year. The vaccine consists of freeze-dried live viruses that have been modified to stop them producing the diseases. The body's defence systems produce antibodies to the diseases to prevent infection at a later date if the person comes into contact with the diseases.

A report in *The Lancet* in 1998 suggested that there was a link between the MMR vaccine and a number of medical conditions including autism. The report was written by Dr Andrew Wakefield, head of the Inflammatory Bowel Diseases Study Group at the Royal Free Hospital. The result was a significantly reduced take-up of the vaccine and an increasing number of measles cases. Measles is, according to the WHO, responsible for the majority of the estimated 1.6 million deaths every year that could be prevented by vaccination. There are over 30 million cases of measles each year worldwide, causing almost 1 million deaths a year. In February 2004, *The Lancet* said that it should not have published the article since the study was flawed and Dr Wakefield had a conflict of interests since he was also carrying out a study on compensation payments for parents of autistic children.

The alternative to the MMR vaccine is separate vaccinations for each of the three diseases. This is more costly, however (and is not available on the NHS), and evidence from countries where this, rather than the single vaccination, is the norm has shown that fewer people finish the complete treatment for all three diseases.

Autism is a condition that leads to intellectual impairment and is usually diagnosed at about the same time as babies receive the MMR vaccination. Most scientific studies do not show any links between the two, but newspaper headlines (and a Channel 5 drama called *Hear the Silence*) have caused considerable concern to parents of new babies. The WHO has stated that 'MMR is recognised by the WHO as having an outstanding safety record and the overwhelming majority of parents still choose MMR as the best way to protect their children. No credible scientific evidence shows an association between MMR and autism.'

More information on MMR can be found on www.mpw.co.uk/getintomed.

HIV/AIDS

To date, about 65 million people have become infected since the disease was first recognized in 1981, and 25 million have died. The number of new infections and deaths is slowing down globally, the result of improved education and the wider availability of treatments. The number of people with HIV who received antiretroviral (ARV) treatment in 2005 was about 1.3 million (although the WHO estimates that there are a further 6.5 million people who require ARV therapy). In the worst affected continent, Africa there is a decline in the number of new infections of up to 25% in six countries within the 15–24 age group. This goes hand in hand with a decline in the rate of sex among young people and the increased use of condoms. However, in some parts of the world, such as Eastern Europe and Central Asia, the number of new infections continues to rise. The table below shows figures for 2005 except where specified otherwise.

Region	Total	New	Deaths	Women
Sub-Sahara	25.8m	3.2m	2.4m	57%
N Africa/ME	510,000	67,000	58,000	47%
S & SE Asia	7.4m	990,000	480,000	26%
E Asia/Pacific	870,000	140,000	41,000	18%
Latin America	1.8m	200,000	66,000	32%
Caribbean	500,000	30,000	24,000	50%
E Europe/C Asia	1.6m	270,000	62,000	28%
W Europe	720,000	22,000	12,000	27%
N America	1.2m	43,000	18,000	25%
Oceania	74,000	8,200	3,600	55%
All (2005)	**40.5m**	**5.0m**	**3.2m**	**46%**
All (2003)	**37.5m**	**4.6m**	**2.8m**	**47%**

Source: World Health Organization

It is estimated that only one in ten of the people who are infected with HIV or AIDS is aware of the fact. In regions where ARV therapy is freely available, there is a significant increase in the number of people who are prepared to undergo HIV/AIDS testing. This has the effect of raising awareness, which in turn reduces the stigma and encourages people to discuss and to confront the disease. This is an important factor in reducing the rate of infection.

It is clear that the only effective way of tackling HIV/AIDS is to adopt sustained and comprehensive programmes in affected areas; short-term measures or individual charities working in isolation have little chance of making a significant impact. The WHO has identified some of the elements that are important in an AIDS/HIV programme:

- Availability of cheap (or free) male and female condoms
- Availability of free ARV therapy
- Availability of effective and free treatment of all sexually transmitted diseases
- Education programmes
- Clear policies on human rights and effective anti-discrimination legislation
- Willingness on the part of national governments to take the lead in the programme.

Currently there are 21 vaccines undergoing trials.

WOMEN AND AIDS

The table on the previous page also highlights the proportion of infection amongst women. In some sub-Saharan African countries more than 75% of young people living with HIV/AIDS are women, and in the sub-Saharan region as a whole the rate of infection among women in the 15–24 age group is over three times greater than that among males in the same age group.

Yet surveys in parts of Zimbabwe and South Africa indicate that nearly 70% of women have only ever had one sexual partner, and education programmes targeting women have been relatively effective. The main cause of the spread of the infection in Africa (and increasingly in India and South-East Asia) is through men having unprotected sex with sex workers and subsequently passing on the disease to their partners. This, in turn, increases the incidences of mother-to-baby infection.

NATURAL DISASTERS

The tsunami in South-East Asia in December 2004 focused the world's attention on the devastation that follows in the aftermath of a natural disaster. The tsunami killed over a hundred thousand people outright, but many thousands more died in the days and months that followed as an indirect result of the waves. Whenever a natural disaster occurs (floods, earthquakes, or other events that displace people from their homes), food supplies are affected and clean water supplies are contaminated, which results in an enormous increase in infectious diseases such as diarrhoea, cholera and typhoid. In addition, malnutrition and difficulties in providing adequate medical treatment contribute to the number of deaths. When flooding occurs there is an increase in the amount of still water, providing breeding grounds for mosquitoes. People in areas that support the anopheles mosquito responsible for malaria face this additional threat.

Natural disasters are not confined to South-East Asia. The earthquake in Pakistan in October 2005 killed 73,000 people, left another 70,000 injured and made 3 million homeless. As well as the problems associated with a lack of clean drinking water, it is estimated that in the three months following the earthquake, 13,000 women delivered babies and many of these mothers and their children needed immediate medical attention.

Even the world's richest and most powerful country, the United States, was unable to cope with the aftermath of Hurricane Katrina, which hit the gulf coast in August 2005 and killed over 1300 people, leaving a further 375,000 homeless.

Man-made disasters, particularly wars and persecution of ethnic groups, also cause people to be displaced from their homes and many of the same problems caused by natural disasters are prevalent.

THE INTERNET

The internet provides the medical world with many opportunities but also some problems. The wealth of medical information available on the internet enables doctors to gain access to new research, treatments and diagnostic methods quickly. Communication between doctors, hospitals, research groups and governing bodies is simple, and news (for example the outbreak of a disease) can be sent around the world in a matter of minutes. The internet can also be used to create web-based administrative systems, such as online appointment booking for patients.

For patients, the internet can be used to find out about treatments for minor illnesses or injuries without having to visit a doctor or a hospital. A good site to investigate is NHS Direct (www.nhsdirect.nhs.uk) which also provides patients with a search engine to locate local doctors.

Not all of the information available, of course, is reliable. Anyone can set up a website and make it appear to be authoritative. Type *cancer*, for example, into Google and you will find nearly 2 billion sites or articles listed! Some of these are extremely useful, such as information sites provided by doctors, health organisations or support groups. However, there is also an enormous number of sites selling medicines or treatments (which, in the best cases, may be harmless but could also be extremely dangerous), and quack remedies. Even if the medication that is purchased is the correct one for the condition, the drugs could be fake, of inferior quality or the incorrect dosage. In many cases, side effects from one type of medication need other drugs to control them.

The internet also allows patients to self-diagnose. The dangers of doing this range from attributing symptoms to something life-threatening (and then buying harmful drugs from another website) to gaining reassurance that the condition is harmless when it might actually be something very serious.

The January 2007 edition of *Student BMJ* featured an article about diagnosis using search engines. Contact details for the *Student BMJ* can be found at the end of this book.

FURTHER INFORMATION

COURSES

INSIGHT INTO MEDICINE
Small-group, two-day courses for sixth-formers in a hospital which allows them to work with doctors, technicians, nurses and volunteer patients to explore the theory, diagnosis and treatment of specific medical conditions such as heart disease. Contact MPW on 0121 454 9637.

MEDISIX
Intensive residential course at Nottingham University School of Medicine, consisting of a series of lectures covering a wide range of medical subjects. There is also a casualty simulation exercise. Tel: 01509 235879 for details.

PUBLICATIONS

CAREERS IN MEDICINE
A Career in Medicine, edited by Harvey White, Royal Society of Medicine Press (www.roysocmed.ac.uk)
Careers in Medicine, Dentistry and Mental Health, Judith Humphries, Kogan Page (www.kogan-page.co.uk)
The Insider's Guide to Medical Schools, Urmston and Calvert, BMJ Publishing Group (www.bmjpg.com)
Medicine Uncovered, Laurel Alexander, Trotman (www.trotman.co.uk)

Learning Medicine, Professor Peter Richards (formerly Dean and Professor of Medicine at St Mary's Hospital Medical School), BMJ Publishing Group (www.bmjpg.com)

MEDICAL SCIENCE – GENERAL

Aspirin, Diarmuid Jeffreys, Bloomsburg

Body Story, Dr David Willham, Channel 4 Books

Catching Cold, Pete Davies, Michael Joseph/Penguin

Don't Die Young, Dr Alice Roberts, Bloomsbury

Everything You Need to Know About Bird Flu, Jo Revill, Rodale

Flu, Gina Kolata, Pan

The Greatest Benefit to Mankind, Roy Porter, Fontana

How We Die, Sherwin Nuland, Vintage

How We Live, Sherwin Nuland, Vintage

The Human Brain: A Guided Tour, Susan Greenfield, Weidenfeld & Nicolson

Human Instinct, Robert Winston, Bantam

Medicine – a History of Healing, ed. Roy Porter, Michael O'Mara Books

Medicine and Culture, Lynn Payer, Victor Gollancz

The Noonday Demon – An Anatomy of Depression, Andrew Solomon, Vintage

Oxford Companion to the Body, Blakemore & Jennett, OUP

The Oxford Illustrated Companion to Medicine, ed. Stephen Lock, John M Last and George Dunea, OUP

Pain – the Science of Suffering, Patrick Wall, Weidenfeld & Nicolson

Penicillin Man – Alexander Fleming and the Antibiotic Revolution, Kevin Brown, Sutton Publishing

Plague, Pox and Pestilence: Disease in History, Kenneth Kiple, Weidenfeld & Nicolson

Poison Arrows, Stanley Feldman, Metro

Practical Medical Ethics, Seedhouse and Lovett, John Wiley

The Secret Family, David Bodanis, Simon & Schuster

Stop the 21st Century Killing You, Dr Paula Baillie-Hamilton, Vermillion

The Trouble with Medicine, Dr Melvin Konner, BBC Worldwide Ltd

User's Guide to the Brain, John Ratey, Abacus

The White Death — A History of Tuberculosis, Thomas
Dormandy, Hambledon
Why We Age, Steven N Austab, John Wiley

GENETICS
The Blind Watchmaker, Richard Dawkins, Penguin
Clone, Gina Kolata, Allen Lane/Penguin Press
Genome, Matt Ridley, Fourth Estate
The Language of the Genes, Steve Jones, Flamingo
The Sequence, Kevin Davies, Weidenfeld & Nicolson
The Single Helix, Steve Jones, Little, Brown
Who's Afraid of Human Cloning?, Gregory and Pence,
Rowman and Littlefield
Y: The Descent of Man, Steve Jones, Bantam

MEDICAL ETHICS
The Body Hunters, Sonia Shah, The New Press
Causing Death and Saving Lives, Jonathan Glover, Penguin

MEDICAL PRACTICE
Bedside Stories — Confessions of a Junior Doctor, Guardian
Books
A Damn Bad Business: The NHS Deformed, Jeremy Lee, Victor
Gollancz
Patient: The True Story of a Rare Illness, Ben Watt, Viking
Patients' Choice, David Cook, Hodder & Stoughton
Medic One On Scene, Dr Heather Clark, Virgin
NHS Plc, Allyson M Pollock, Verso
Repeat Prescription — Further Tales of a Rural GP, Dr Michael
Sparrow, Robinson

HIGHER EDUCATION ENTRY
BMAT: Preparation for the BMAT, Heinemann
CRAC Degree Course Guides: Medical and Related Professions,
Trotman (www.trotman.co.uk)
Degree Course Offers, Brian Heap, Trotman
Getting into Oxford & Cambridge, MPW Guides/Trotman
(www.trotman.co.uk)
How To Complete Your UCAS Application, MPW
Guides/Trotman (www.trotman.co.uk)

Mature Students' Directory, Trotman (www.trotman.co.uk)
University and College Entrance: The Official Guide, UCAS

WEBSITES

All the medical schools have their own websites, (see below) and there are numerous useful and interesting medical sites. These can be found using search engines. Particularly informative sites include:

Admissions forum: www.admissionsforum.co.uk (essential information for applicants)

BMAT: www.bmat.org.uk

British Medical Association: www.bma.org.uk

Department of Health: www.open.gov.uk/doh

General Medical Council: www.gmc-uk.org

Student BMJ: www.studentbmj.com

UKCAT: www.ukcat.ac.uk

World Health Organization: www.who.int

FINANCIAL ADVICE

For information on the financial side of 5–6 years at medical school see www.money4medstudents.org. This has been prepared by the Royal Medical Benevolent Fund, in partnership with the BMA Medical Students Committee, the Council of Heads of Medical Schools and the National Association of Student Money Advisers.

EXAMINERS' REPORTS

The examining boards provide detailed reports on recent exam papers, including mark schemes and specimen answers. Schools are sent these every year by the boards. They are useful when analysing your performance in tests and mock examinations. If your school does not have copies, they can be obtained from the boards themselves. The examining boards' addresses are:

www.aqa.org.uk
www.edexcel.org.uk
www.ocr.org.uk
www.wjec.co.uk

CONTACT
DETAILS

STUDYING IN THE UK

Aberdeen
Carol Baverstock
Head of Admissions
Kings College
Aberdeen University
Aberdeen AB24 3FX
www.abdn.ac.uk/medicine

Birmingham
Professor Chris Lote
Associate Dean (Admissions)
The Medical School
Birmingham B15 2TT
www.medicine.bham.ac.uk

Brighton and Sussex
John Kay
Admissions Tutor
Brighton and Sussex Medical School
Mithras House
Lewes Road
Brighton BN2 4AT
www.bsms.ac.uk

Bristol
Melanie Stodell
Admissions Officer
Faculty of Medicine
University of Bristol
Senate House
Tyndall Avenue
Bristol BS8 1TH
www.medici.bris.ac.uk

Cambridge
Head of Cambridge Admissions Office
Kellet Lodge
Tennis Court Road
Cambridge CB2 1QJ
www.medschl.cam.ac.uk

Cardiff

Admissions Officer
Medical School Office
Wales College of Medicine, Biology, Life and Health
  Sciences
Cardiff University
Heath Park Campus
Cardiff CF14 4XN
www.cardiff.ac.uk/medicine

Dundee

Mr Gordon Black
Admissions Officer
Admissions and Student Recruitment
University of Dundee
Dundee DD1 4HN
www.dundee.ac.uk/medicalschool

Durham

Admissions Office
Queen's Campus Stockton
University Boulevard
Stockton on Tees TS17 6BH
www.dur.ac.uk/phase1.medicine/welcome.htm

East Anglia

Dr D Heyling
Admissions Tutor
School of Medicine
University of East Anglia
Norwich NR4 7TJ
www.med.uea.ac.uk

Edinburgh

Dr Neil McCormick
Undergraduate Admissions Officer
The Medical School
Teviot Place
Edinburgh EH8 9DF
www.mvm.ed.ac.uk

Glasgow

Anne Cooney
Admissions Secretary
Medical School
University of Glasgow
Glasgow G12 8QQ
www.gla.ac.uk/faculties/medicine/index.html

Hull York

Connie Cullen
Hull York Medical School
York University
Heslington
York YO10 5DD
www.hyms.ac.uk

Imperial College

David Gibbon
Admissions Officer
School of Medicine
Imperial College of Science, Technology and Medicine
London SW7 2AZ
www.ic.ac.uk/medicine

Keele

Julia Molyneux
Admissions Administrator
School of Medicine
Keele University
Staffordshire ST5 5BG
www.keele.ac.uk/depts/ms

King's College London

Martyn Annis
Assistant Registrar (Admissions)
Student Admissions Office
King's College London
Hodgkin Building
Guy's Campus
London SE1 1UL
www.kcl.ac.uk/depsta/medicine

Leeds

Ann Gaunt

Sub-Dean for Admissions

University of Leeds Medical School

Worsley Building

Leeds LS2 9JT

www.leeds.ac.uk/medicine

Leicester

Dr Kevin West

Senior Tutor for Admissions

Maurice Shock Medical Science Building

University Road

Leicester LE1 9HN

www.le.ac.uk/sm/le

Liverpool

Jane Goldberg

Admissions Officer

Faculty of Medicine

Duncan Building

Daulby

Liverpool L69 3GA

www.liv.ac.uk/medicine

Manchester

Mrs Linda Harding

Admissions Officer

University of Manchester Medical School

Stopford Building

Oxford Road

Manchester M13 9PT

www.medicine.manchester.ac.uk

Newcastle

Mrs D Smith

Admissions Officer

The Medical School

Framlington Place

Newcastle upon Tyne NE2 4HH

http://medical.faculty.ncl.ac.uk

Nottingham

Martine Lowes

Admissions Officer

Medical School

University of Nottingham

Queen's Medical Centre

Nottingham NG7 2UH

www.nottingham.ac.uk/mhs

Oxford

Dr Catherine Hawkins

Pre-Clinical Studies Office

Medical Sciences Teaching Centre

South Parks Road

Oxford OX1 3RE

www.medsci.ox.ac.uk

Peninsula Medical School

Sue Locke

Senior Undergraduate Admissions Administrator

Peninsula Medical School

ITTC Tamar Science Park

Davy Road

Plymouth PL6 8BX

www.pms.ac.uk

Queen Mary (Barts and the London)

Sarah Tattersall

Head of Admissions

Barts and the London School of Medicine and Dentistry

Turner Street

London E1 2AD

www.smd.qmul.ac.uk

Queen's Belfast

Mr S Wisener

Admissions Officer

Queen's University Belfast

Northern Ireland BT7 1NN

www.qub.ac.uk/cm

Sheffield
Anna Berridge
Medical Admissions Officer
Faculty of Medicine
Beech Hill Road
Sheffield S10 2RX
www.shef.ac.uk/medicine

Southampton
Dr Jenny Skidmore
Admissions Tutor
School of Medicine
Biomedical Sciences Building
Bassett Crescent East
Southampton SO16 7PX
www.som.soton.ac.uk

St Andrews
Dr David Jackson
Medical Admissions Officer
Admissions Application Centre
79 North Street
St Andrews
Fife KY16 9AJ
http://medicine.st-and.ac.uk

St George's
Ms Caroline Persaud
Admissions Officer
St George's Hospital School of Medicine
Cranmer Terrace
London SW17 0RE
www.sgul.ac.uk

Swansea
Admissions Office
School of Medicine
Grove Building
University of Wales, Swansea
Singleton Park
Swansea SA2 8PP
www.medicine.swan.ac.uk

UCL (and Royal Free)

Dr Brenda Cross
Sub-Dean and Faculty Tutor
Royal Free & University College Medical School
University College London
Faculty of Life Sciences
Gower Street
London WC1E 6BT
www.ucl.ac.uk/medicalschool

Warwick

Lesley Ling
Senior Admissions Assistant
University House
University of Warwick
Coventry CV4 8UW
www2.warwick.ac.uk/fac/med

ACCESS TO MEDICINE

Derek Holmes
The College of West Anglia
Tennyson Avenue
King's Lynn
Norfolk PE30 2QW
01553 761144 (ext 309)

STUDYING OUTSIDE THE UK

M & D Europe (UK) Ltd (for English-language
courses in the Czech Republic and the Cayman Islands)
Challenge House
616 Mitcham Road
Croydon CR0 3AA
0871 717 1291
www.readmedicine.com

Royal College of Surgeons in Ireland

123 St Stephen's Green
Dublin 2
Ireland
www.rcsi.ie

Margaret Lambert
St George's University School of Medicine
University Centre
Grenada
www.sgu.edu
0800 169 9061 (from the UK)

TABLES

TABLE 1: MEDICAL SCHOOL STATISTICS FOR 2006 ENTRY

	Applied	Interviewed	Offers
Aberdeen	1,773	584	321
Birmingham	2,589	932	852
Brighton & Sussex	2,568	461	242
Bristol	2,007	~700	Not available
Cambridge	1,392	Not available	306
Cardiff	2,888	889	558
Dundee	1,533	350	280
Durham	Included within Newcastle figures		
East Anglia	1,710	497	270
Edinburgh	3,077	60	366
Glasgow*	1,321	854	476
Hull York	1,192	495	339
Imperial	~3,000	716	508
Keele	1,010	505	266
King's	3,500	1,000	640
Leeds	2,882	782	463
Leicester	2,131	1,000	400
Liverpool*	1,854	1,080	830
Manchester	3,101	1,183	685
Newcastle	2,992	795	605
Nottingham	~1,800	750	494
Oxford	~1,000	~400	160
Peninsula	1,874	699	346
Queen Mary	2,760	1,097	619
Queen's Belfast	765	38	360
Sheffield	3,280	890	578
Southampton	3,320	205	389
St Andrews	1,096	375	324
St George's	2,193	850	349
UCL	2,215	800	550

*Note: Figures for graduate-entry programmes are excluded. *Figures for 2003 entry.*

VOLUNTEERING

Positive East (HIV/AIDS voluntering)
159 Mile End Road
London E1 4AQ
www.positiveeast.org.uk

Accepted	Clearing	Graduates	Resits
168	0	36	0
372	0	18	1
136	Not available	Not available	Not available
217	Not available	19	Not available
288	0	Not available	Not available
450	0	7	0
157	0	20	0
	Included within Newcastle figures		
163	0	77	Not available
228	0	13	0
248	0	37	0
142	0	29	0
326	0	14	6
110	0	31	18
320	0	48	Not available
237	0	19	5
200	0	Not available	6
315	Not available	32	Not available
401	0	16	0
381	0	11	0
227	0	5	0
157	0	Not available	Not available
191	6	22	Not available
277	0	Not available	Not available
261	0	13	4
335	0	42	11
203	0	11	0
161	0	8	Not available
190	0	Not available	Not available
330	0	50	Not available

TABLE 2: MEDICAL SCHOOL ADMISSIONS POLICIES FOR 2008 ENTRY

	Usual offer	Usual AS requirements
Aberdeen	ABB	Biol
Birmingham	AAB	B in Biol
Brighton & Sussex	AAB	Biol + Chem
Bristol	AAB	Biol
Cambridge	AAA	3rd science/Maths
Cardiff	AAB	Biol + Chem; B in Biol/Chem if not at A2
Dundee	AAA	Biol
Durham	Same as for Newcastle	
East Anglia	AAB; Access encouraged	B in 4th AS
Edinburgh	AAA	Biol; B in 4th AS
Glasgow	AAB	Biol
Hull York	AAB	B in 4th AS
Imperial	AAA	B in 4th AS
Keele	AAB	Chem; B at GCSE in non-AS sciences
King's	AAB	Biol + Chem; C in 4th AS
Leeds	AAB	Not specified
Leicester	AAB	Biol
Liverpool	AAB	B in 4th AS (Gen St accepted)
Manchester	AAB	Not specified
Newcastle	AAA	If only 1 of Biol and Chem at A2/AS, other at GCSE
Nottingham	AAB	AA in Biol + Chem
Oxford	AAA	Not specified
Peninsula	AAB–ABB	C in 4th AS
Queen Mary	AAB	Biol + Chem
Queen's Belfast	AAA	Biol; A in 4th AS
Sheffield	AAB	Chem + Biol + Maths/Phys + 1 other
Southampton	AAB	B in Chem/Biol
St Andrews	AAB	GCSE Biol + Maths if not at AS/A2
St George's	ABB–BBC	Biol + Chem; B in 4th AS
UCL	AAB	B in Biol

Note: Details were correct when going to press – check websites for updated information. For Swansea and Warwick, see section on mature students on page 70.

Usual A2 requirements	Retakes considered?*
Chem + 1 other science/Maths	No
Chem + 1 other science/Maths	In extenuating circumstances and if narrowly missed AAB
Biol/Chem	Yes
Chem + 1 other science/Maths	In extenuating circumstances
Chem + 1 other science/Maths	In extenuating circumstances
Biol/Chem	If previously applied to Cardiff
Chem + 1 other science/Maths	In extenuating circumstances
Biol	Yes
Chem + 1 other science	In extenuating circumstances
Chem + 1 other science/Maths	In extenuating circumstances
Biol + Chem	Yes
Biol/Chem	In extenuating circumstances and if previously applied to Imperial
Biol/Chem + 1 other science/Maths	Yes – see prospectus
Biol/Chem	In extenuating circumstances
Chem	In extenuating circumstances
Chem	In extenuating circumstances and if previously held Leicester offer
Biol + Chem	In extenuating circumstances
Chem + 1 other science	If previously applied to Manchester
Biol/Chem	In extenuating circumstances
Biol + Chem + 1 other science	In extenuating circumstances
Chem + 1 other science	In extenuating circumstances
A in 1 science	Yes
2 sciences inc Biol/Chem	In extenuating circumstances
Chem + 1 other science/Maths	If previously held Queen's offer and missed by 1 grade
AB in Chem + 1 other science/Maths	Yes
Biol/Chem	In extenuating circumstances and if retaking 1 subject
Chem + 1 other science/Maths	No
Biol/Chem	No
Chem	If held UCL offer and achieved BBB

*Note: Retake candidates will normally be expected to achieve AAA.

TABLE 3: INTERVIEW AND WRITTEN TEST POLICIES FOR 2008 ENTRY

	Typical length	Panel No	Members	Test
Aberdeen	20 mins	2–3	ABCDFGHJ	UKCAT
Birmingham	15 mins	3	BCDEF	None
Brighton & Sussex	20 mins	3	CDFGH	UKCAT
Bristol	15 mins	2	ABCDFGH	None
Cambridge	2 x 20 mins	2–3	BCDFG	BMAT
Cardiff	20 mins	2–3	ABCDEFGJ	UKCAT
Dundee	20 mins	2	FHJ	UKCAT
Durham	20 mins	2	ABCFGHIJ	UKCAT
East Anglia	40 mins	7*	CD	UKCAT; case history to discuss
Edinburgh	30 mins	3	G	UKCAT
Glasgow	15 mins	2	ACDFG	UKCAT
Hull York	20 mins	2	CF	UKCAT; short article to comment on
Imperial	15 mins	4	BCEFG	BMAT
Keele	15 mins	4	CDFG	UKCAT
King's	15 mins	2	BCDF	UKCAT; 20-min questionnaire
Leeds	20 mins	3	ABCDEFGHIJ	UKCAT
Leicester	15 mins	2	CE	UKCAT
Liverpool	15 mins	2	ACDFGI	None
Manchester	15 mins	4	CDFG	UKCAT
Newcastle	20 mins	2	ABCFGHIJ	UKCAT
Nottingham	15 mins	2	ABCDFGH	UKCAT
Oxford	2 x 20–30 mins	2–4	CF	BMAT; UKCAT (graduates)
Peninsula	20 mins	3–4	DFHJ	UKCAT; 20-min questionnaire
Queen Mary	15 mins	3	ABCDEFGHJ	UKCAT; video
Queen's Belfast	15 mins	3	DFH	UKCAT
Sheffield	20 mins	3	CDEFIJ	UKCAT
Southampton	20 mins	2	ABCDFGH	UKCAT
St Andrews	20 mins	2	ABCDFGHJ	UKCAT
St George's	15–20 mins	4	ABCDEFGHJ	UKCAT
UCL	15–20 mins	3	ABCDEFGHJ	BMAT

*Each interviewer has 5 minutes with candidate. **A**: admissions dean / associate dean; **B**: admissions tutor; **C**: doctor from medical school; **D**: doctor from local area; **E**: medical student; **F**: member of academic staff; **G**: member of admissions committee; **H**: administrator; **I**: member of trust board; **J**: other healthcare professional.

POSTSCRIPT

If you have any comments or questions arising from this book, the staff of MPW and I would be very happy to answer them. You can contact us at the addresses given below.

Good luck with your application to medical school!

James Burnett

MPW (London)
90/92 Queen's Gate
London SW7 5AB
Tel: 020 7835 1355
Fax: 020 7225 2953
enquiries@mpw.co.uk